Supporting the Well Being of Girls

An evidence-based school programme

Tina Rae and Elizabeth Piggott

 Routledge
Taylor & Francis Group

LONDON AND NEW YORK

First published 2014
by Routledge
2 Park Square, Milton Park, Abingdon, Oxon OX14 4RN

and by Routledge
711 Third Avenue, New York, NY 10017

Routledge is an imprint of the Taylor & Francis Group, an informa business

British Library Cataloguing in Publication Data
A catalogue record for this book is available from the British Library

Library of Congress Cataloging-in-Publication Data
Rae, Tina.
  Supporting the well being of girls: an evidence-based school programme / Tina Rae, Elizabeth Piggott.
     pages cm
  Includes bibliographical references and index.
  1. Girls–Education. 2. Girls–Psychology. 3. Educational psychology. 4. Educational evaluation. I. Piggott, Elizabeth. II. Title.
  LC1481.R34 2014
  371.822–dc23   2013050199

ISBN: 978-1-138-01525-8 (hbk)
ISBN: 978-1-138-01526-5 (pbk)
ISBN: 978-1-315-79452-5 (ebk)

Typeset in Helvetica
by Keystroke, Station Road, Codsall, Wolverhampton

Printed and bound by CPI Group (UK) Ltd, Croydon, CR0 4YY

Contents

Image credits

Appendix 12.2   Victoria Pendleton © Featureflash | Dreamstime.com
Appendix 13.1   Young Builder © Hpphoto | Stock Free Images
Appendix 14.2a   Mother's time © Luis Louro | Dreamstime.com
                     Child puffing a cigar © Dunca Daniel | Dreamstime.com
Appendix 14.2b   Mother and child © Edwardje | Dreamstime.com
                     Little girl with Christmas hat and wine glass © Imagery Majestic |
                     Dreamstime.com

Foreword

I am extremely proud to be able to write this foreword for a publication which I know will have enormous relevance to girls and young women in today's complex society. Given the fact that young people appear to be more at risk than ever before of developing issues around self-esteem, self-concept and overall well being this is certainly a timely and much needed resource. Dr Tina Rae, with the assistance and support of innovative staff from The Springfields Academy where I am the principal, initially created 'The Extreme PSD Curriculum'.

This was also a timely piece of work in terms of supporting the overall development and mental health needs of our school population.

Whilst motivating, challenging and inspiring, this refreshing new approach to education has subsequently delivered life-transforming results for some of our most complex and disaffected students.

Using twenty-first-century media technology and exciting out of the classroom experiences, determination, courage and equality are all social skills you can see evolve and embed in the students' characters as a result of their participation.

Alongside this project it was also deemed essential that we particularly focus upon the needs of our small group of more vulnerable girls. Hence the development of a discrete programme which was also clearly informed by Tina's research in the London borough of Merton and elsewhere. I know that this is a truly valued programme and will no doubt ensure that girls and young women from a range of educational and social contexts will engage with the resources, and benefit hugely from participating in these very relevant and engaging sessions.

Tina – thank you for taking on this project and creating a groundbreaking approach to such an important aspect of education and for inspiring others such as Elizabeth to take the journey with you.

Trystan Williams
Principal
The Springfields Academy

Acknowledgements

Tina and Elizabeth would like to acknowledge the contributions of Liz Burns, Holly Worts, Tracey Johnstone and Liane Whiteley in the delivery and development of this programme. They would also like to thank the students of The Springfields Academy.

Introduction

The research

During the last 2 years research has been conducted into the topic of girls' pressures and issues in the London Borough of Merton. Dr Tina Rae worked with colleagues in order to identify a group of girls and young women who were presenting with a range of behaviours which were felt to be putting them at risk – both emotionally and physically – in a wide range of contexts. She was keen to explore the reasons and contributory factors and to also ensure that the girls' views were elicited. The general discourse around these young women appeared to be one of negativity in that they were regarded as putting themselves at risk due to their daily behaviour and apparent self-harming behaviours.

Feedback from staff within the local authority had also highlighted concerns regarding early sexualisation of these students and a range of substance abuse which seemed to put them at risk from males and also engaged them in negative patterns of self-harming behaviours which militated against personal and educational progression and development. It was evident to school-based staff at the outset of the work undertaken at The Springfields Academy that these issues had enormous resonance for them in terms of their approaches and concerns in working with girls and young women in the specialist context.

Literature review

Although girls have been outperforming boys in terms of academic achievement for the last 20 years, there does remain a concern regarding the specific achievements of white working-class pupils from both genders. Nationally, it is this group who are less likely to stay on in education and training (DfES, 2003) or enter higher education (Archer *et al.*, 2003). There are also increasing concerns regarding the challenges faced by girls from within this vulnerable group and the problems that they seem to face in today's increasingly complex and highly sexualised society. Concerns have increasingly been raised regarding the sexualisation of girls and the impact that this has on self-esteem, attitudes and behaviour within relationships, and academic performance and achievement.

Impact of the media

The media provides ample evidence of the sexualisation of women, including music videos, television, magazines, films, music lyrics, sports media, video games, internet and advertising (Gow, 1996; Gruerholz & King, 1997; Krassas *et al.*, 2001; Lin, 1997;

Plous & Neptune, 1997; Vincent, 1989; Ward, 1995). Studies which focus upon the media indicate very strongly that women as opposed to men are more frequently portrayed in a sexual fashion and are also subsequently objectified. These media images also further emphasise a narrow and unrealistic notion of physical beauty which has evident implications for the development of self-esteem and self-image of girls and young women (O'Donohue *et al.*, 1997).

Pressure through interpersonal relationships

Girl's relationships can also be seen as a source of sexualisation. Parents/carers may present girls and young women with the message that being physically attractive is one of the most important goals for them to achieve and some will also provide access to plastic surgery in the attempt to reach the ideal (Brown & Gilligan, 1992). Research also shows that teachers can encourage girls to play at being sexualised adult women (Martin, 1998) or maintain the belief that girls from specific ethnic backgrounds are hypersexual and therefore unlikely to achieve any real academic success in school (Rolon-Dow, 2004).

It is also evident that both male and female peers contribute to this process. Peer pressure from both genders has been found to contribute to girls conforming to standards of thinness or sexiness (Eder, 1995; Nichter, 2000). A key concern is also the particular ways in which the process encourages boys to sexually objectify and harass girls. This kind of behaviour is also 'normalised' by the girls themselves via the process of self-objectification – the process whereby girls and young women learn to think of and treat themselves as objects of other people's (mainly boys' and men's) desires (Fredrickson & Roberts, 1997; McKinley & Hyde, 1996).

The impact of sexualisation

The unrealistic expectations on girls and young women to achieve the 'ideal' in terms of appearance has led to an increase in eating disorders and the number of young women having breast implants at an increasingly early age (Zuckerman & Abraham, 2008). Exposure to gender-stereotypical ideas and images also contributes to sexist attitudes and beliefs and sexual harassment and violence against women (Kilbourne & Lazarus, 1987). Sexual objectification can also be seen to enable and encourage a range of oppressions including employment discrimination and sexual violence alongside the trivialisation of women's roles and accomplishments in the workplace (Fredrickson & Roberts, 1997).

The mainstreaming of the sex industry has also led to an increase in the number of girls and young women entering careers such as lap dancing or glamour modelling which require a 'sexy' image (Deeley, 2008) whilst the viewing of sexually objectifying images of young women has also led to more acceptance of violence within relationships (Kalof, 1999; Lanis & Covell, 1995). The increasing availability of pornography via advances in technology has also been seen as a contributory factor to the increase in acceptance of sexual aggression within relationships (Malamuth *et al.*, 2000).

Possible implications

The report of the American Psychological Association's (APA) task force (2007) on the sexualisation of girls concludes that it is vital for psychologists, educators, carers and community organisations to work together in order to encourage the development of curricula which enhance self-esteem based upon young people's abilities and character as opposed to their appearance. The report also advocates increasing public awareness and the development of policy in this area in order to reduce sexualised images of girls in all forms of media and products and the development of positive portrayals of girls and young women as strong, competent and non-sexualised.

Rationale and research objectives and context of the study

Such objectives formed the basis and the rationale of this current study in which the researchers aimed to highlight the impact of sexualisation and sexual objectification upon girls and young women within this particular London local authority context. The initial anecdotal feedback from school-based staff to the educational psychologists involved revealed increasing concerns as to the apparently 'unsafe' nature of some of the girls' behaviours, and the negative impact upon self-image, self-esteem, achievement and interpersonal relationships. It was hoped that the study would elicit and highlight the girls' own concerns and realities regarding their own lives alongside perhaps suggesting some useful strategies or frameworks for developing positive support mechanisms for the future.

Method

A qualitative research paradigm that espoused an open-ended exploratory nature, using focus groups as a method of data collection was employed. Convenience sampling was used in relation to the schools and the selection of the participant students.

Participants

The characteristics of the participants are summarised in Table 1.

Table 1 Characteristics of the participants

Focus group	Number of participants	Ethnicity	Gender	Year group
1	5	White British	female	10
2	5	White British	female	10
3	6	5 White British and 1 Black Afro-Caribbean British	female	10
4	6	White British	female	6
5	4	White British	female	6
6	4	White British	female	6

Procedure

Focus groups were undertaken with the participants by two of the researchers.

A key function of focus groups is to gain views on products, programmes, services and institutions (Stewart & Shamdasani, 1998). They are basically semi-structured interviews with the added value of interaction in a group, with the discussion being focused around one identified theme (Krueger, 1994).

Millward (1995) demonstrated that focus groups can enhance the ability of psychologists to answer research questions and generate questions from new angles and perspectives, i.e. they provide for a broad, exploratory tool in the early stages of the research which, in turn, can inform the later stage, i.e. interview content.

The use of the focus group in this study was important in ensuring that insights were gained that might be less likely to surface in the one-to-one interview context (Morgan, 1998). According to Willig & Stainton-Rogers (2003) the particular strength of such groups lies in the nature of the interactions generated as, 'statements are challenged, extended, developed, undermined or qualified in ways that generate rich data for the researcher' (Willig & Stainton-Rogers, 2003: 29).

The questions posed were as follows:

- Do you think 'girls' are at risk?
- What does being at risk mean to you?
- Are they more at risk than boys? If so what are girls doing that is putting them at risk/in danger?
- When do things go wrong for girls? When do they need help?
- How could schools help young girls to be safer? Happier?
- Is it important for women to work to have a career?
- Should girls have careers and should they progress?
- Are they equal to men?
- How important is school?
- Should women be financially independent of men?
- How do culture/media impact on you? How do the images you see in the press and on TV make you feel and think and behave?
- What's important in life? Is life a quest for happiness? Are we entitled to be happy? What does being fulfilled mean?
- Who do you respect as a woman? Who wouldn't you respect and why? Role models – who are they? Who are these people who have it all?
- Why do people engage in risky or self-harming behaviours like taking drugs or belonging to gangs? What causes them to do this and what influences the way they do or do not cope?
- What do you think can be done to monitor, control or prevent bullying? What do you think would or does work?
- Do you ever feel lonely or stressed and what helps you?
- What is your definition of a good 'girlfriend'?

Data collection and analysis

Each focus group was recorded and saved as an audio file which was subsequently transcribed as a Word document. The Word documents were combined to represent an entire data set, rather than a subset of the data for the purposes of analysis. The rationale for this was to provide key themes that reflected the entire data set highlighting the commonalities of particular themes. The data was coded using an inductive thematic analysis (Braun & Clarke, 2006) approach to analysis that allowed the development of categories and themes directly from the data. This ensured that all views, including those not anticipated, were reflected in the reporting of the findings.

Findings

In this study, it has been possible to identify general themes, and to describe patterns across data via a 'bottom up' data-driven approach as described above. In brief, the themes identified were as follows:

Theme 1: Safety issues

It was recognised that girls were generally less safe and more vulnerable to crime than boys when they were on the streets and that they sometimes made themselves more vulnerable by dressing in revealing clothes which might attract attention.

The risk of being raped was mentioned in the majority of focus groups as were the difficulties faced by girls in trying to get home safely after drinking and socialising in general.

Theme 2: Relationships

The difficulties faced by girls from within their own relationships with each other were mentioned in all focus groups and peer pressure and relational aggression were described as key issues and concerns.

The pressure to have sex was also highlighted and also the concern around the fact that boys would expect girls to behave in the same way as women they had observed via pornographic material on the internet.

Bullying of girls by both genders was perceived to be a major concern in all focus groups.

Theme 3: Media pressures

The pressure to look good and achieve the so-called 'airbrushed' ideal was highlighted in all focus groups and the fact that boys particularly expected girls to match up to such images was a real cause for concern.

Theme 4: Valuing education/careers

The importance of education as a means of achieving success in the workplace was highlighted alongside the difficulties faced by girls feeling trapped in their own contexts and helpless in terms of breaking out and achieving real success.

The fact that the media tends to focus on celebrity culture and does not always show successful women who have and are working hard to achieve and be successful was also raised.

Theme 5: Financial independence

Being financially independent of men was deemed to be a good thing in terms of being able to make your own choices and decisions and particularly important should there be a breakdown in the relationship.

Theme 6: Happiness/well being

Happiness was equated with feeling good about oneself, having positive relationships with significant others and enough money to live reasonably well and without too much stress.

Ways of coping with stressful relationships or events ranged from self-harm as a coping mechanism at one end of the continuum to strategies emanating from positive psychology at the other.

Theme 7: Role models

Many of the participants identified celebrities as being role models but generally in a negative sense. Those who had overcome or encountered difficulties were deemed to be more positive role models and the majority of participants cited their mothers or other significant female family members as role models for them.

Conclusions of the study

The findings of this study have illustrated that there are a range of factors that impact upon girls and young women as they attempt to negotiate their roles within a complex and often challenging social context. Together, these factors pose a challenge to both the girls and young women concerned and also to those who support them in both the social and learning contexts. The key factors can be summarised as follows:

- Girls and young women feel less 'safe' than boys and young men in the social context
- Boys are identified as 'bullying' girls and as having unrealistic expectations as to how girls should look and behave due to airbrushed and sexualised images in the media and pornographic content on the internet
- Relational aggression between girls and young women is an issue and concern on a regular basis and school systems for dealing with bullying of this nature are seen to be inadequate
- Girls and young women feel a continual pressure to conform to an ideal image of beauty as presented in the media and the stress associated with this can impact negatively on self-esteem and become the root cause of self-harming behaviours
- Girls and young women recognise the value of education in terms of future job satisfaction and financial independence whilst also feeling constrained by low expectations and misogynistic attitudes within their home contexts

- Girls and young women equated happiness and well being with 'feeling good about yourself' and identified stress as mainly stemming from pressures of school work, pressures (from both genders) to look good and to 'have a boyfriend' and cited listening to music as a means of coping
- The majority of girls and young women in this study cited their mothers/female family members as being good role models and were dismissive of celebrities who they perceived to be 'fake' in terms of both their behaviour and appearance.

These findings support those of earlier research studies which highlight how the media provides a great deal of evidence for the sexualisation of girls and young women and the resulting objectification they then engage in (Gow, 1996; Gruerholz & King, 1997; Krassas *et al.*, 2001; Lin, 1997; Plous & Neptune, 1997; Vincent, 1989; Ward, 1995). The negative impact of these images on girls' behaviour, self-esteem and self-image in terms of emphasising a narrow and unrealistic notion of physical beauty is also consistent with previous research (O'Donohue *et al.*, 1997). The findings also highlight how peer pressure from both genders promotes conformity with standards of 'thinness' and 'sexiness' (Eder, 1995; Nichter, 2000). The ways in which this process encourages boys to sexually objectify and harass girls is also consistent with previous studies as is the self-objectification undertaken by these students (Fredrickson & Roberts, 1997; McKinley & Hyde, 1996).

In addition, these results also provide a particular insight into the ways in which girls and young women feel constrained and pressured not only by peers and sexualised and idealised images in the media but also by their own social contexts. There is evidence here of the power of the constraints placed upon them from within a misogynistic home context and the ways in which they feel limited in terms of 'escaping' from stereotyped roles and behaviours in the future.

Implications of findings and the role of staff in 'social, emotional and behavioural difficulties' contexts

It is hoped that the findings of this research will be utilised by the local authority to develop a guidance document for schools which can be considered to be evidence based. This will focus upon the ways in which the sexualisation of girls and young women is addressed and tackled at a whole-school level and the ways in which positive images of girls and young women as strong, competent and non-sexualised are provided both in the curriculum and at a systemic level within the school context.

Most importantly for this publication, these findings also help to form the evidence base for the development of a curriculum for girls and young women attending a range of educational contexts which focuses upon:

- Gender awareness and equality
- Positive peer relationships
- Confidence, self-esteem and safety of girls and young women
- Management of stress, peer pressure and relational and sexual bullying
- Awareness of sexualisation in both the media and social and learning contexts
- Skills and strategies to assertively highlight and tackle sexualisation and misogyny in both the social and learning contexts
- The promotion of positive role models

- Teenage relationship abuse
- Well being and 'happy habits'.

Well being

As the development and maintenance of well being is central to this programme of support it is important to further consider this concept. So, what is it that actually constitutes mental health and well being? The DfES (2001) adopted the Mental Health Foundation's definition of children's mental health, describing the mentally healthy child as one who can:

- Develop psychologically, emotionally, intellectually and spiritually
- Initiate, develop and sustain mutually satisfying personal relationships
- Use and enjoy solitude
- Become aware of others and empathise with them
- Play and learn
- Develop a sense of right and wrong
- Resolve (face) problems and setbacks and learn from them.

This list is further built upon by Helpguide (www.helpguide.org/mental-emotional-health.htm) to also include:

- A sense of well being and contentment
- A zest for living – the ability to enjoy life, laugh and have fun
- Resilience – being able to deal with life's stresses and bounce back from adversity
- Self-realisation – participating in life to the fullest extent possible, through meaningful activities and positive relationships
- Flexibility – the ability to change, grow and experience a range of feelings as life's circumstances change
- A sense of balance in one's life between solitude and sociability, work, play, sleep and wakefulness and rest and exercise
- A sense of well-roundedness with attention to mind, body and spirit
- Creativity and intellectual development
- The ability to care for oneself and others
- Self-confidence and self-esteem.

On initial reading, this list may appear somewhat simplistic. However, once we begin to reflect upon our own lives and relate these descriptors to young people in schools, it is possible to see how it can provide an initial starting point for identifying problems and difficulties. As Prever (2006) states, 'They are also useful indicators when we consider their opposites – an activity that way gives us some insight into the meaning of mental health problems and mental illness' (p. 10).

Raising awareness

When quoting the Office for National Statistics (2000) Young Minds noted that over 10 per cent of children aged between 5 and 15 years are affected by a mental health problem and that this figure rises to 11.2 per cent for students of statutory secondary school age. They further calculate that the average secondary school of 1,000 pupils will have:

- 50 students with depression
- 10 affected by eating disorders
- 100 suffering/experiencing 'significant distress'
- 10–20 students with obsessive compulsive disorder
- 5–10 attempting suicide.

Although such figures may well be described by some as a medicalisation of behavioural problems, they do remain a significant concern for those working with young people in schools. As Prever suggests, 'This, then, is the task faced by schools. Wherever possible, we need to find ways to prevent these problems in young people from developing. We need to act early with our own school-based support systems and refer on to – and work directly with – mental health professionals where this is felt necessary and desirable' (2006: 13). It is also important to highlight the fact that such statistics would be significantly higher within the special school context in which students have identified social, emotional and behavioural difficulties alongside a range of co-morbid complex features.

Risk and resilience effect

In the first instance, identifying students most at risk can perhaps best be done via reference to the risk and resilience factors detailed in Tables 2 and 3. The DfES (2001) suggested that these 'risk' factors are cumulative, i.e. when a young person faces more risk than resiliency factors then significant difficulties are far more likely to develop.

Table 2 Risk factors

Individual	Family	Community
Genetic factors	Overt parental conflict Family breakdown	Socioeconomic disadvantage
Low intelligence	Inconsistent or unclear discipline	Disaster
Learning difficulties	Hostile and rejecting relationships	Homelessness
Communication difficulties	Failure to adapt to a child's changing needs	Discrimination
Academic failure	Physical/sexual/emotional abuse	Other significant life events
Difficult temperament	Parental criminality, alcohol/substance misuse	
Low self-esteem	Death and loss – including loss of friendship	
	Parental illness	

British Association for Counselling and Psychotherapy (BACP) (2005)

Table 3 Resilience factors		
Individual	**Family**	**Community**
Being female	At least one good parent–child relationship	Wider supportive network
Higher intelligence	Affection	Good housing
Easy temperament as an infant	Supervision	Higher standard of living
Secure attachment	Authoritative discipline	High morale in school
Positive attitude/ ability to problem solve	Support for education	Schools with strong academic and non-academic opportunities
Religious faith	Supportive partnership/ absence of severe discord	Range of positive sport and leisure activities
Humour Capacity to reflect		
Good communication skills		
British Association for Counselling and Psychotherapy (BACP) (2005)		

However, when students are identified in this way, it is then vital for staff to implement the appropriate support systems/mechanisms. These may range from referral to specialist agencies at one end of the continuum to the development of individualised and group programmes to build resilience and the key skills of emotional literacy. Teachers can and do successfully prevent the escalation of mental health problems in young people by understanding more about these protective factors and ensuring that they are promoted at an individual, group and systems level across the whole school community.

School protective factors

So, what are these protective factors within the school context? The British Association for Counselling and Psychotherapy (BACP) (2005) list these as follows:

- At least one significant and caring relationship with an adult in school
- High expectations of academic success
- High behavioural expectations and firm and clear boundaries
- Positive school climate and high morale among staff and pupils
- Extensive extracurricular programme including sports
- Opportunity for active participation in the life of the school
- Curriculum that is structured, thematic and experimental
- Curriculum that recognises that children learn in different ways
- Concern for promoting the self-esteem, independence and self-efficacy of pupils
- Teachers offering time and space to listen
- School providing welfare, mentoring and counselling as part of the formal pastoral system

- Teachers and other adults in school model caring relationships and communication
- School encouraging young people to have a sense of connectedness and belonging
- Pupils valued equally regardless of difference
- Schools demonstrating commitment to physical and emotional health, and healthy lifestyles and sexual attitudes encouraged
- Conflict managed well
- Pupils' achievement valued and celebrated
- Clear policies on anti-bullying and drug misuse
- Well-established programmes in personal and social education and citizenship
- Active sex education policy and programme for personal relationships and sex education
- Caring, empathic teachers and support staff
- Teachers showing genuine interest in and concern for pupils' learning and well being
- School providing professional development opportunities for staff
- Teacher encouragement of the development of prosocial behaviour
- School encouraging parental involvement
- School making opposition to injustice and discrimination explicitly clear.

Establishing our programme – a child-centred model

This Girls' curriculum aims to promote well being by building positive relationships within a nurturing and child-centred approach. This builds upon resilience factors and protective factors within the school context.

As highlighted previously, access to a supportive network can function as a protective factor, supporting and promoting resiliency within a community context, to combat severe risk factors such as homelessness. In a school context, protective factors such as having at least one significant and caring relationship with an adult; clearly being a school which demonstrates concern for and commitment to pupils' self-esteem, well being, independence, self-efficacy and emotional health; and school teachers who freely offer time and space to listen, can impact positively upon the resiliency of young people.

It was these findings which informed the development of a child-centred approach. The main tenets of the model adopted include taking into account the individual needs of each member, looking at the reasons behind different behaviours rather than reacting to the behaviours themselves, and promoting the right of the young person to choose and communicate, whilst accepting these choices and not basing judgements upon them.

The practitioners believed from the outset that persistently adhering to this model would result in the formation of trusting and respectful relationships between all group members, and that once such relationships had begun to form the young people could then begin to recognise their negative behaviours and practise change within a context where they felt protected from negative judgement.

Issues in multi-agency working and the development of a joint approach between clinicians and teachers

When developing this programme, practitioners thought that there was potential for tension between the needs and expectations of the senior management team in terms of educational and behavioural boundaries and expectations and the clinical staff in terms of their therapeutic approach as described above. They felt that clear and open communication, trust and respect of professional expertise would be required to prevent conflict and achieve professionally appropriate approaches and outcomes.

Historically, it is evident that leaders and managers need to be aware of group dynamics to enable everyone within a multi-agency team to have a say, get involved and have their particular contribution identified and valued. Issues which arise can be addressed proactively as part of the induction process or through introductory or ongoing training, for example by:

- initiating discussions of inevitable issues which arise in multi-agency groups
- asking the whole staff to discuss what would be unacceptable behaviours related to group working
- using these as part of the 'ground rules' for working together
- using exercises and case studies to tackle issues in group dynamics.

The crucial role of management was highlighted in the *National Evaluation of Children's Trusts* (University of East Anglia and National Children's Bureau, 2005). Managers would need to acknowledge practitioners' professional roles and expertise, protect professional boundaries, allocate cases according to the skills of staff in multi-agency teams and trust professionals within their teams. They would also need to balance recognition of the distinct skills and expertise of the different professionals in their teams with a requirement for common skills.

The team at our pilot school originally identified two school-based counsellors and an Assistant Psychologist to work with the Consultant Educational Psychologist to develop the programme and agree the approach. The adoption of the child-centred approach as described above did subsequently result in some tension in the area of behaviour management and expectation. There was a sense that teaching staff were less comfortable with what they perceived to be an 'unboundaried' forum, with girls having the freedom to move around and express themselves using inappropriate language. This was seen by the clinicians as key to ensuring the development of confidence, self-expression and feelings of ultimate safety within the clinical relationship. For school-based teaching staff the concerns remained, however, around how 'in control' the clinicians were of the process and in ensuring the safety and behaviours of the girls in line with school-based expectations.

There was some evidence of a tension between those adhering primarily to a strong behaviourist tradition and those who were aiming to incorporate clinical systems and what they perceived to be more emotionally intelligent approaches. In effect, the challenge was how to make the clinical intervention 'fit' with the educational approach. In order to attempt such innovative practice and to begin to ensure that staff could successfully work together in order to do this, it was agreed that the team be broadened to incorporate members of the care team – one of whom also had experience in teaching. The programme could then be developed and delivered by these members of staff working as a team and ensuring the 24-hour curriculum for girls could be further developed within this residential setting. Agreeing that the clinical principles and approaches would be maintained within a more boundaried context ensured that school expectations regarding behaviour were adhered to. This would involve regular meetings to ensure the development of the programme and its sustainability with both younger and older groups of girls and young women being targeted in separate interventions. This ongoing dialogue would then ensure agreed approaches and content of the sessions and 24-hour curriculum activities which ensured the well being of girls within this context. It would also provide a forum for transparent working and approaches which would also ensure that all staff – both clinical and teaching/care staff – could operate within a safe and purposeful framework agreed by all.

Overall aims of the programme

The aim of the programme is to build a therapeutic environment that allows and promotes autonomy, emotional resilience and open communication. This statement can be broken down into three main objectives:

1 Promote emotional resilience within the group members
2 Assist in the develop of the skills associated with positive communication
3 Support group members with a view to further developing self-regulation.

The sessions

Each of the sessions for students is presented in the form of a chapter in this book. The sessions are as follows:

1 Introduction
2 Self-esteem
3 Body image and appearance
4 Stereotypes
5 Relationships part 1
6 Relationships part 2
7 Bullying
8 Mental health
9 Anxiety and depression
10 Stress
11 Self-harm part 1
12 Self-harm part 2
13 Using therapeutic tools from CBT
14 Parenting
15 Healthy living
16 Looking forward/evaluation.

The session structure

The sessions are generally structured as follows, although there are some differences between the sessions:

Welcome

At the beginning of each session the students should be welcomed into the room. They are also informed of the session title, and a very brief outline of what they will be doing is given.

Group rules

Practitioners should agree on certain rules before the first session. For example as the sessions are likely to involve discussions about challenging, emotive and personal issues, it is advisable to remind all group members to be mindful of confidentiality. Another group rule could involve 'safe places'. Again because of the subject matter, students may occasionally become uncomfortable; therefore it may be advisable for students to have access to agreed places which they can withdraw to for a few moments if they wish.

At the beginning of each session attention should be drawn to these rules. This helps remind the students of the boundaries that are in place. Students should also be given the opportunity to amend any of the group rules during this interval, for example they may wish to add words or phrases to the list of unacceptable language.

Talk time

During this time students should be invited to share any ideas or suggestions they may have regarding the current session, and to review their week, focusing on both positive and negative occurrences.

Points should be listened to, taken note of and acted upon. At the beginning of each talk time the students should be reminded that as the curriculum is run solely for the benefit of the students involved, it is important that they get out of it what they need. Because of this the students should be allowed to lead any discussions which occur during talk time. They should feel comfortable in the knowledge that if they wish to discuss an issue, this time provides them with an appropriate context in which to do so.

Talk time is extremely important during the first few sessions as it is an essential component in developing respectful and trusting relationships between the students and facilitators. It is essential for the students to understand that if they offer feedback regarding previous sessions it will be recognised.

The inclusion of this interval is intended to encourage the students to listen to each other and the facilitators, learning to offer and accept gentle challenges and differences of opinions. It is hoped that this will help a collective sense form within the group and strengthen relationships within.

Icebreaker

This interval often comprises a short activity designed to encourage the students to communicate with one another and the practitioners. They are also designed to bring the students together within the context of the 'group'.

This may help reduce any anxieties surrounding participation that the students might have. For this reason the activities are often light hearted. The introduction to a session may also involve a general discussion surrounding the session title or its key themes.

Core activity/activities and additional activities

The majority of each session is given over to a core activity or activities. Whether the core activity is broken down into two activities depends upon the session topic and the nature of the activities themselves. If the session covers challenging topics then often two activities are included to allow for a break in between. Students may benefit more from this break time if it is spent outdoors, even if it just involves a brisk walk.

These core activities may sometimes involve written tasks which can be discussed amongst the group in the first instance so that the students can then fill in their own individual activity sheets to store in their folders. This method can be beneficial to those students who lack confidence in their literacy skills as they may feel more confident sharing their thoughts and feelings verbally with the group. It is also important to remember to present activity sheets and activities at a level that is relevant and accessible to the students.

Reflections and feedback

During this interval students should be encouraged to voice any opinions they may have regarding the session. Not only is this beneficial in helping to shape future sessions but it may also help to instil reflexive practice and self-evaluation within the facilitators and the students.

It also provides the students with an opportunity to reflect on the learning that has taken place.

Target setting

For each session a target should be set for completion during the coming week. This encourages the students to use, practise and develop the skills they learn from the curriculum outside of session time.

Compliments to close

Each session should conclude with an exchange of positive remarks. These can be about the session, or about another group member. It is likely that many of the students will struggle with praise, therefore trying to encourage them to accept positive feedback is very important. It is also important for the facilitator to have skills in providing such feedback in a stepped and empathic manner which facilitates a growing acceptance of compliments and positive comments over time. Our key tip here would be to start small and then to build up the praise and never to indulge inauthentic praise whereby a 'false' compliment is given to a young person.

Relaxation

Each session should finish with a relaxation technique. It is hoped that by doing this the students will be able to experience a range of different strategies and techniques used to help aid relaxation, and that eventually they will find one that will benefit them.

A few points to note

It is very important that the facilitator(s) make themselves aware of the contents and aims of each of the sessions in the programme so as to ensure that their selection (if they choose not to deliver all of the sessions in sequence) is entirely appropriate to the target group. It may be appropriate to select a more targeted set which focuses on key areas such as relationships or self-image. This will also need to be planned with time constraints in mind as some institutions may not be able to allocate sufficient time in any one or two terms to be able to deliver all of these sessions in sequence.

It should also be noted that the images selected for the programme to date have been done so with groups of girls currently in mainstream and special education within the UK. These may well not be entirely suitable or appropriate in other contexts and it may be necessary to source alternative images which have more meaning and relevance to the specific group of girls being targeted. The existing framework and contents of the sessions will remain pertinent; it is simply that the facilitator(s) will have to source some additional images at some points in the course of delivering the programme.

THE PROGRAMME

Chapter 1
Introduction

Resources required

- Flip chart for group rules
- Selection of 'female-interest' magazines
- Doughnuts – enough for one per group member
- Thought diaries printed up and bound ready for decoration
- Arts and crafts materials with which to decorate the diaries

The objective of the first session is to communicate the key aims and the contents of the curriculum with the students involved. The expectations of and reasons for participation should also be discussed.

It is important that this communication is shared. Students should be offered the opportunity to communicate their wishes and expectations for the curriculum to the facilitators.

Group rules

It is here that the group rules should be drawn up and recoded (possibly using the format provided **(Appendix 1.1)**). Start with those set by the practitioners and then invite the students to offer their own. It is important that attention is drawn to these group rules at the beginning of each session. They should be visible at all times so that they can be referred to throughout the session. A set of group rules may include the following statements:

Everyone should try to keep bad language to a minimum.
Everyone should try not to use any of the banned words.
Everyone should ask permission before taking a time out.
Everyone should recognise that what is talked about in these sessions should stay in these sessions.
Everyone needs to listen to each other and not talk over one another.
Everyone needs to try to give ideas and offer solutions.
Everyone must be careful not to criticise others' ideas but to build upon them.

Talk time

In this first session it is important to emphasise to the students that this interval will become a regular feature of every session. Facilitators may also wish to highlight the importance of 'chat time' with other women.

As it is likely that any discussion in this session will focus on the curriculum itself, perhaps the facilitators could frame this talk time in the form of a thought storm activity using the activity sheet provided **(Appendix 1.2)**.

Introduction

This time should be spent welcoming the students to the session. It is likely that on arrival the students will be both apprehensive and inquisitive. In order to reassure them, the rationale behind the inception of the curriculum should be explained and understood. It may be helpful for the facilitators to highlight the following points:

This is a group for girls which will focus upon the key issues and challenges they face.
Topics we will cover include relationships, bullying, self-esteem, stress, self-harm and healthy living.
There will be regular opportunities within these groups to discuss things that concern you within a supportive environment.

Icebreaker

This first icebreaker is titled 'Which celebrity inspires you the most?' To begin spread a number of 'female-interest' magazines out over the table and prompt the students to pick one image of a celebrity they are inspired by. Proceed round the table, taking it in turns to present the images and discuss the reasoning behind their selection. This activity is intended to ease the students into the session and to encourage them to begin to partake in group discussions.

Core activity (a)

This activity is intended to show the students that participation in this curriculum will also be enjoyable. The 'Doughnut game' should be played by both the facilitators and the students. In pairs, one person should attempt to eat a doughnut without licking their lips. Their partner should watch carefully to see how long it takes before they inevitably do so. During feedback the following questions could be considered:

Did you realise you were licking your lips?
Was it difficult to stop licking your lips?
Do you do other things without thinking?
Can you tell us what you do without thinking?
How could you stop yourself doing these things?

Core activity (b)

During the first session this time should be used to introduce the students to their thought diaries **(Appendix 1.3)**. These diaries provide the students with a place to record their thoughts and feelings as the weeks progress. It is advisable to have the diaries printed and bound prior to the session, ready for the students to personalise and decorate. Arts and crafts materials (e.g. pens, glitter, sequins) with which to do this should be provided. A suggested layout for the thought diaries is shown in **Appendix 1.3**.

Each diary page also includes space for the students to write and record their F.U.F.s for each week. F.U.F. stands for 'fortunately, unfortunately and fortunately'. In order to complete the F.U.F.s section of their thought diaries the students have to look back over the previous week and identify one positive occurrence. When noting down they should begin their sentence with 'fortunately'. They then identify one negative occurrence and should begin their sentence with 'unfortunately'. They then finish with another positive occurrence, again beginning their sentence with 'fortunately'. We have offered an example below:

Fortunately, as its Friday the weekend is nearly here.
Unfortunately, my Granddad is ill.
Fortunately, he is in high spirits and is showing signs of improvement.

Structuring thoughts like this helps the students to evaluate their week, identifying both positive and negative events. During the first session it should be made clear that students are free to discuss F.U.F.s with the group *if they wish*. If they do not feel comfortable with this then it is more than acceptable for them not to share with anyone, including practitioners.

Reflections and feedback

The students should be given the opportunity to offer any feedback they may have regarding this session. Facilitators could also encourage students to reflect on the learning that has taken place, using the following conversation prompts:

Was the first session similar to what they expected?
How do they feel about the coming weeks and sessions?
Are there any changes or suggestions they would like to make now that the first session is drawing to a close?

Target setting

The target for the coming week is to 'christen' the thought diaries **(Appendix 1.3)** with their first entry. The entry can be as big or as small as the students wish. The students should also be reminded that they are not expected to share their entry with the group next session but can do so if they wish.

Compliments to close

This section aims to provide each of the students with a positive piece of feedback. It will be important for the facilitator to ensure that each student is given a compliment by another student member of the group or one of the facilitators. Such compliments could involve highlighting the following behaviours:

Listening well.
Showing empathy or concern for others.
Being thoughtful.
Working hard in activities during the session.
Acknowledging the contributions made by others.
Overcoming any initial embarrassment or fear and trying to contribute.
Having a go and being positive in the session.

It may be helpful to reinforce these positives by nominating a Very Important Player at the end of each session. The facilitators could award this to students who they feel performed well during the session. A picture or sticker could be cut out and stuck into the student's thought diary as a reminder of the positive contribution they have made to the group.

For this first session the facilitators may wish to include a more structured activity in this section. In this case each member of the group could be provided with a sheet of plain paper, a marker pen and a piece of tape. The students could then be asked to record compliments and positive comments about each individual group member on these sheets which are stuck onto their backs. Once this has been completed and everyone has contributed to everyone else's compliment sheets, the students can then read through these positive comments. It may be useful to allow some time for the students to consider how this activity makes them feel. Facilitators could use the following conversation prompts:

Do you feel positive about what you have just read?
Or do you feel embarrassed?
Do you feel as if your self-esteem has been reinforced or do you feel slightly uncom-
    fortable?

Considering why they should experience such feelings may also be part of this reflection process.

It may also be useful to ask the students to provide some positive feedback regarding the session itself. Students may need to be prompted in order to offer a positive remark. If this is the case, something as simple as 'was the session as bad or as boring as you expected?' could be used to encourage conversation.

Relaxation

Learning to relax is an important life skill. Those of us who forget about the importance of relaxation are prone to illness, depression, anxiety and exhaustion. Therefore each session will include time to try out different relaxation techniques. These can often be quite informal. For example, the technique for this session is flicking through the magazines used during the icebreaker whilst sharing hot chocolate and biscuits.

Additional activities

X-treme problems!

The two activity sheets in **Appendix 1.4** feature two scenarios in which a girl is experiencing a difficulty or problem, presented in the form of an 'agony aunt' letter. The students could be asked to consider one or both of these problems in turn and what advice they might offer to the 'writer'. They could also consider ways in which the writer might find a solution to the dilemma and how they might deal more effectively with the problem. Central to this activity is the need to ensure that all students feel able to participate. If some students are reluctant to write their own responses, one of the facilitators could record key themes and ideas which come out of the group discussions on the format provided **(Appendix 1.5)**. This way the activity could be kept entirely verbal.

The key aim is to encourage students to articulate thoughts and feelings; it does not matter whether this articulation is written or verbal. Given that they are not being identified as personally experiencing this problem, it is hoped that students will feel more inclined to discuss the feelings that the character in each of the scenarios may be experiencing and to offer solutions, i.e. developing empathy en route.

Who supports me?

This activity sheet **(Appendix 1.6)** is intended to gather information specific to each student. Students could be asked to complete the activity sheet by placing the names of those people who they believe provide them with support within the concentric circles. Those figures who provide the most support should appear within the innermost circles as the closer the name appears to the centre circle the more support is perceived. It is incredibly useful for the facilitators to be aware of the extent and nature of each student's support structure. This information will benefit the facilitators during future discussions. This activity is also beneficial to the students as it enables them to really think through and acknowledge the supportive individuals who they have around them.

'Supporting the Well Being of Girls' group rules

Appendix 1.1

What are the issues faced by girls today?

My thoughts

	Weekly target
F	
U	
F	

Appendix 1.3

X-treme problems!

HELP!

Everyone is being so unreasonable! They all hate me because sometimes I take things that I want. It's like if I want it, I'll just take it. I'm getting pretty good at it too!

I'd never steal from my friends or my mum and dad, mostly I just nick from the shops and they can afford it! There not going to miss the odd chocolate bar!!! I love the excitement and don't want to stop. How do I get everyone off my back?

Appendix 1.4a

X-treme problems!

Dear Agony Aunt,

I'm not sure what I should do! I think I have feelings for my best friend's boyfriend!!! I love spending time with him and I love it when he pays me more attention than her.

I'm worried that if we are alone together we might end up kissing. Should I tell her? Shall I stop spending time with both of them? Please help me, I don't want to lose her as a friend but I don't see any other way!

Appendix 1.4b

Dear Reader,

➡️

➡️

➡️

➡️

➡️

Appendix 1.5

Who supports me?

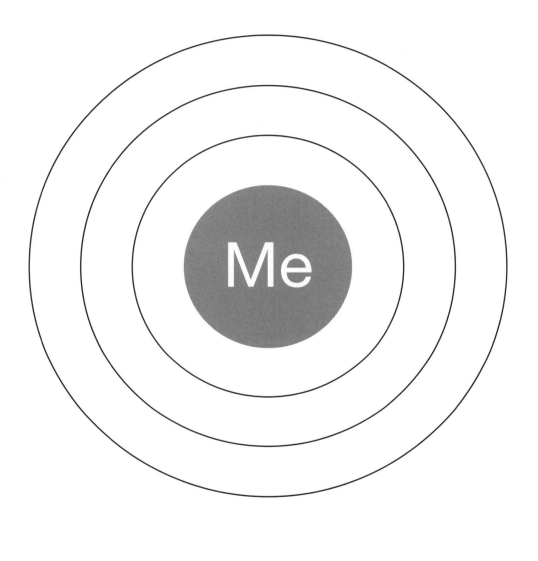

Me

Appendix 1.6

Chapter 2
Self-esteem

Resources required

- Flip chart for group rules
- Inflated balloons, cocktail sticks and felt-tip pens
- Copies of the 'Resiliency builders' questionnaire, enough for one per student
- Copies of the '14 ways . . . to enhance self-esteem' information sheet
- CD and CD player, or laptop with adjustable volume
- Colouring pens, pencils and colouring sheets

The objective of this second session is to introduce the topic of self-esteem. Hopefully by the end of the session, students will be well on their way to formulating their own definitions and ideas about the concept.

Self-esteem has always been a vital area for development in young people, and one that has been frequently misunderstood and even demonised by some members of the psychological community. Why is it so important? *'It is because children learn well with a combination of appropriately high expectations and appropriately high self-esteem'* (Roberts, 2002). In order to develop this appropriate level of self-esteem, learners need to be able to take risks; this process must involve failure and the need for young people to be able to cope with the associated frustration. We therefore need to focus on preventing students from engaging in a negative learning cycle, for example: I worry about failing – I will not succeed – I won't bother trying.

It is important, at the same time, to note that the relationship between academic achievements and self-esteem is rather confusing. Does good self-esteem raise achievement or does achievement raise self-esteem? This is rather a chicken and egg concept. What is evident, however, is the fact that children who believe in their abilities tend to achieve more, i.e. the notion of the self-fulfilling prophecy.

KEY TERMS

There is some confusion about the key terms of *self-concept*, *ideal self*, *self-esteem* and *global self-esteem*.

- *Self-concept or self-image* is really the perception that a child has of himself – how he defines himself. For example: I'm a boy; I'm Arthur's best mate; I play football; I like Big Macs. My self-concept would be that I am a woman; I am loyal; I like writing and going to the gym; I love good wine and malt whiskey. It's these individual components that make up the person.
- The *ideal self* is what or who I would really like to be, and this is usually an idea that is formulated in comparison to others.

- *Self-esteem*, in effect, is the evaluation of those parts. It is a personal judgement of worthiness based on the above. For example, how much do I value being Arthur's mate? How important is it to have friends?
- *Global self-esteem* is the overall feeling that we have towards ourselves. There will be specific areas where we feel good about ourselves and others where we're not so positive – this is perfectly normal.

Group rules

At the beginning of each session the group rules should be revisited. The students should be asked if they wish to make any alterations or additions to these rules. It is important that students are able to refer to these throughout the session, therefore they should be placed somewhere in the room where they will remain visible for the duration.

Talk time

As the students don't have another opportunity during their school week to get together in an 'all-female' environment this time should be used primarily to 'catch up'. It could also be used to review the previous session and to introduce the topic of this current session.

This talk time also presents the facilitators with an opportunity to introduce the picture portraits. Proposed layouts for these can be found in **Appendix 2.1**. In order to create their picture portraits each student will need a large sheet of white card (preferably A2). These will also have to be personalised. If they wish to, students can place a photo or a picture of themselves in the centre of the card, or they can simply write their names. These picture portraits will be used in a number of future sessions as a place to record achievements and other positive notes. For example, during this session students could be asked to pick a positive point about themselves, and write it on one of the sticky shapes provided. This could then be stuck on to their picture portraits.

Icebreaker

The facilitator(s) can present each student with a choice of coloured balloons and ask them to draw a face on it which represents how they are currently feeling. If their mood changes at any time during the session the students should feel free to pop their balloon and replace it with another which represents their new emotion. It is hoped that this will encourage the students to 'take the time out' to think about the emotions they are experiencing and to recognise and acknowledge changes in mood.

Introduction

By way of an initial introduction to the concept, students could be provided with the following definitions:

High self-esteem – a positive evaluation of your worthiness and value as an individual, which is both enabling and empowering.

Low self-esteem – a negative evaluation of your worthiness and value as an individual, which is expressed in the attitudes you hold towards yourself.

Self-esteem has many causes and can be linked to distorted self-evaluation. Teasing or bullying by peers can trigger attachment issues which often lead to an inferiority complex. Low self-esteem is also frequently caused by a poor ability to communicate, which limits the success of a student's social interactions. What is important to remember, however, is that experiencing low self-esteem at some point in our lives is completely normal. This is not a problem if we have what Rob Long (2009) calls 'a reservoir of good feelings to ourselves in order to help heal ourselves'.

The students can be asked to identify three good feelings that they have about themselves and that others have about them which can and do help them to remain upbeat when things get tough. They can then be encouraged to focus on the following questions:

How have I done as well as I've done?
What are the two or three biggest challenges, including crises or traumas I've overcome in my life?
What did I use to overcome them?

Core activity (a)

It is essential that young people learn how to develop their own personal resiliency builders in order to overcome adversity. Individual qualities that facilitate resiliency are as follows:

- Relationships
- Humour
- Inner direction
- Perceptiveness
- Independence
- Positive view of personal future
- Flexibility
- Love of learning
- Self-motivation
- Competence
- Self-awareness
- Spirituality
- Perseverance
- Creativity.

It is important for individuals to recognise the personal resiliency builders that they use most frequently. Do they rely upon relationships and the ability to be a friend and form a positive relationship? Do they use humour to deflect difficult situations and feelings? Are they able to adjust to change, and bend as necessary in order to positively cope with a range of situations? Are they able to use creative outlets in order to express themselves? Building this kind of self-awareness is particularly important when young people are developing in all these areas. They require prompting to consider their skills and to reflect upon how they can be further developed.

The students can be asked to reflect upon their own skills by completing the 'Resiliency builders' questionnaire **(Appendix 2.2)**.

Core activity (b)

It is useful to provide students with the following 14 ways to enhance self-esteem. These are common sense strategies, clearly not rocket science – but it can be all too easy to forget the importance of such simple ideas:

- Spend time with people who like you and care about you.
- Ignore and stay away from people who put you down or treat you badly.
- Do things that you enjoy or that make you feel good.
- Do things you are good at.
- Reward yourself for your successes.
- Develop your talents and skills.
- Be your own best friend and treat yourself well doing things that are good for you.
- Make choices for yourself and don't let others make those choices for you.
- Take responsibility for yourself, your choices and your actions.
- Always do what you believe is right.
- Be true to yourself and your values.
- Respect other people and treat them right.
- Set goals and work to achieve them.

And, finally and most importantly:

- Don't beat yourself up when you get it wrong.

These can be presented as an information sheet **(Appendix 2.3)** and each idea discussed in turn. Do the students agree with these suggestions? Would they work for them? If so, how? If not, why not?

Reflections and feedback

The students should be given the opportunity to offer any feedback they may have regarding this session. Facilitators could also encourage students to reflect on the learning that has taken place, using the following conversation prompts:

What did you make of our first topic covered?
Have you learnt anything about self-esteem that you didn't know already?
How does self-esteem differ from self-image?
What steps can you take to promote your own self-esteem?

Target setting

Students could be asked to record two positive statements and one negative statement about themselves using the F.U.F. format demonstrated in Chapter 1. A proposed example could be:

Fortunately, I'm a very loyal friend.
Unfortunately, I'm not very good in a crisis.
Fortunately, I'm not afraid to 'muck in' when something needs doing.

Compliments to close

This section aims to provide each of the students with a positive remark. It will be important for the facilitator to ensure that each student is given a compliment either by themselves or by another student member of the group.

As mentioned previously, students could be asked to identify a positive point about themselves to write on one of the sticky shapes provided. This could then be stuck onto their picture portraits. They could also identify a positive point about another group member which could subsequently be stuck onto their picture portraits.

Relaxation

The technique for this session is calm colouring. The students should have access to relaxing music and colouring pens, pencils and colouring sheets to allow them to 'doodle' whilst the music is playing. A calm colouring format is provided **(Appendix 2.4)**.

Additional activities

Who am I?

This activity sheet is intended to assist the students in exploring the concept of self-image. One way of beginning to understand your own self-image is to ask yourself the question 'who am I?' twenty times. The facilitators could help the students to complete the 'Who am I???' activity sheet **(Appendix 2.5)** by offering the following statements as examples:

I am a little sister.
I work at this school or college.
I am a Geordie.
I am below average in height.
I have a very low tolerance for alcohol.

Break the cycle . . .

This additional activity attempts to change the way the students think about a perceived personality trait. It may be helpful to first show the students the 'Break the cycle . . .' information sheet **(Appendix 2.6)** which includes an example of a negative automatic thought cycle. The facilitators should talk the students round the cycle, explaining how the individual arrives at each thought. The students could then be asked if they recognise this pattern. Do they follow this pattern when they think negatively about themselves? If so, they could be asked to complete their own version of the cycle using **Appendix 2.7**, which follows the same format as before. The 'Negative automatic thoughts' activity sheet **(Appendix 2.8)** attempts to encourage the students to challenge these thoughts by looking at the evidence for each one. For example, the evidence for someone being terrible at keeping in touch with friends is that they often go for weeks without speaking to some of them. But of course this is easily addressed simply by picking up the phone! Once the students begin to evaluate these negative thoughts they will hopefully begin to think of ways to break them. Once they have done this they will be able to reframe and neutralise the negative automatic thoughts.

To finish this activity it may be advisable to focus on some positive thoughts, as these can follow the same automatic cycle as negative thoughts. Students could be asked to complete the 'Think positively!' activity sheet **(Appendix 2.9)** using their own example. The following subheadings have been omitted from the positive automatic thought cycle in an attempt to really get the students thinking:

Positive thought – Makes you like and approve of yourself – Produces positive feelings – Causes you to behave in a positive way – Confirms positive thoughts.

The following could be used as an example if it is required:

I'm good at football – I feel talented, special even – football is a positive thing to be good at which makes me feel good about myself – I always go to football practice and put in the maximum effort – I'm getting even better!

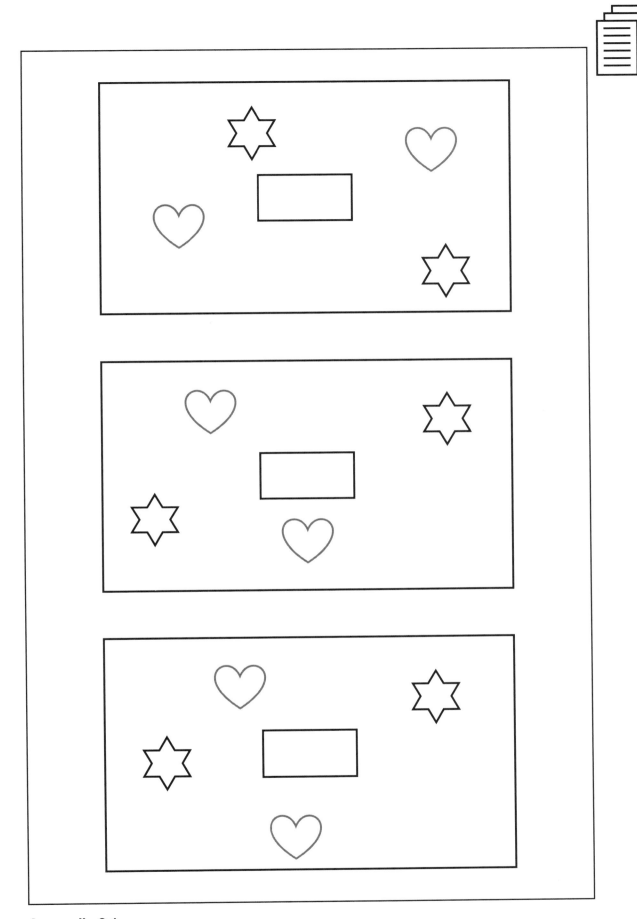

Appendix 2.1

Resiliency builders

**Tick against the top 3 or 4 resiliency builders that
you use most often**

**Tick
here**

	1	RELATIONSHIPS	Sociability/ability to be a friend/ability to form positive relationships
	2	HUMOUR	Has a good sense of humour
	3	INNER DIRECTION	Bases choices/decisions on internal evaluation (internal locus of control)
	4	PERCEPTIVENESS	Insightful understanding of people and situations
	5	INDEPENDENCE	'Adaptive' distancing from unhealthy people and situations/autonomy
	6	POSITIVE VIEW OF PERSONAL FUTURE	Optimisim; expects a positive future
	7	FLEXIBILITY	Can adjust to change; can bend as necessary to positively cope with situations
	8	LOVE OF LEARNING	Capacity for, and connection to learning
	9	SELF-MOTIVATION	Internal initiatives and postive motivation from within
	10	COMPETENCE	Is 'good at something'/personal competence
	11	SELF-WORTH	Feelings of self-worth and self-confidence
	12	SPIRITUALITY	Personal faith in something greater
	13	PERSEVERANCE	Keeps on despite difficulty; doesn't give up
	14	CREATIVITY	Expresses self through artistic endeavour

STOP, THINK AND REFLECT

- How have you used these in the past/how do you currently use them?
- How can you best apply them to current life problems?
- Which resiliency builders could you add to your personal repertoire?

Appendix 2.2

14 ways...

to enhance self-esteem

Spend time with people who like you and care about you.

Ignore and stay away from people who put you down or treat you badly.

Do things that you enjoy or that make you feel good.

Do things you are good at.

Reward yourself for your successes.

Develop your talents and skills.

Be your own best friend and treat yourself well doing things that are good for you.

Make choices for yourself and don't let others make those choices for you.

Take responsibility for yourself, your choices and your actions.

Always do what you believe is right.

Be true to yourself and your values.

Respect other people and treat them right.

Set goals and work to achieve them.

And, finally and most importantly

Don't beat yourself up when you get it wrong.

Appendix 2.3

Calm colouring

Appendix 2.4 Calm colouring

Who am I???

How would you describe yourself, what are you like?

1.

2.

3.

4.

5.

6.

7.

8.

9.

10.

11.

12.

13.

14.

15.

16.

17.

18.

19.

20.

Appendix 2.5

Break the cycle...

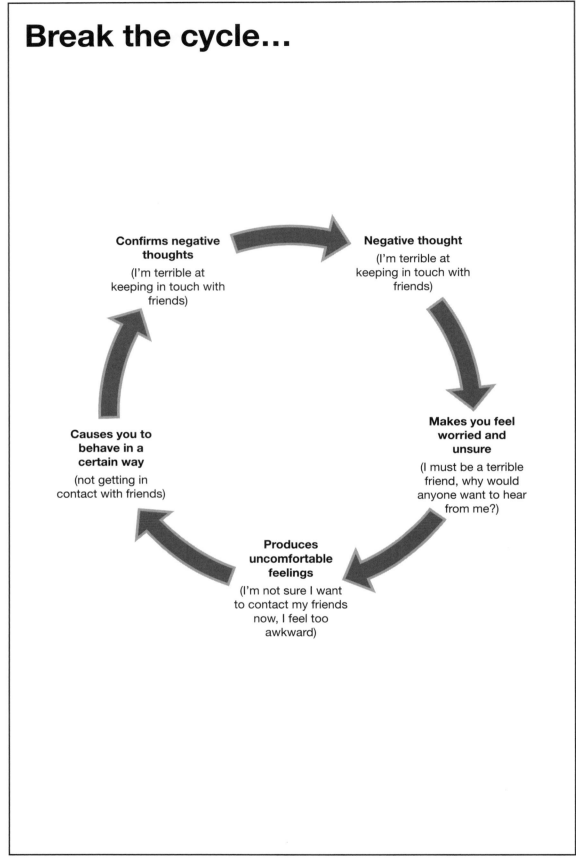

Confirms negative thoughts

(I'm terrible at keeping in touch with friends)

Negative thought

(I'm terrible at keeping in touch with friends)

Makes you feel worried and unsure

(I must be a terrible friend, why would anyone want to hear from me?)

Causes you to behave in a certain way

(not getting in contact with friends)

Produces uncomfortable feelings

(I'm not sure I want to contact my friends now, I feel too awkward)

Appendix 2.6

Try and have a go yourself...

Confirms negative
thoughts

Negative thought

Makes you feel
worried and
unsure

Produces
uncomfortable
feelings

Causes you to
behave in a
certain way

Appendix 2.7

Negative automatic thoughts (or NATs!)

We need to challenge our negative thoughts and always check out the evidence! How true are these thoughts and how can we change negative thoughts in to more balanced thoughts? Have a go at reframing these NATs. The first one is done for you!

I'm terrible at keeping in touch with friends

Evidence: I often go weeks without speaking to some of my friends

I may not talk to my oldest friends as much as I would like but they are still my oldest friends for a reason! And when we do get together it's like we've never been apart!

I always get left out

I can't do this activity

I never look as good as the other girls

My work is never as good as the others

I always misbehave

Appendix 2.8

Think positively...

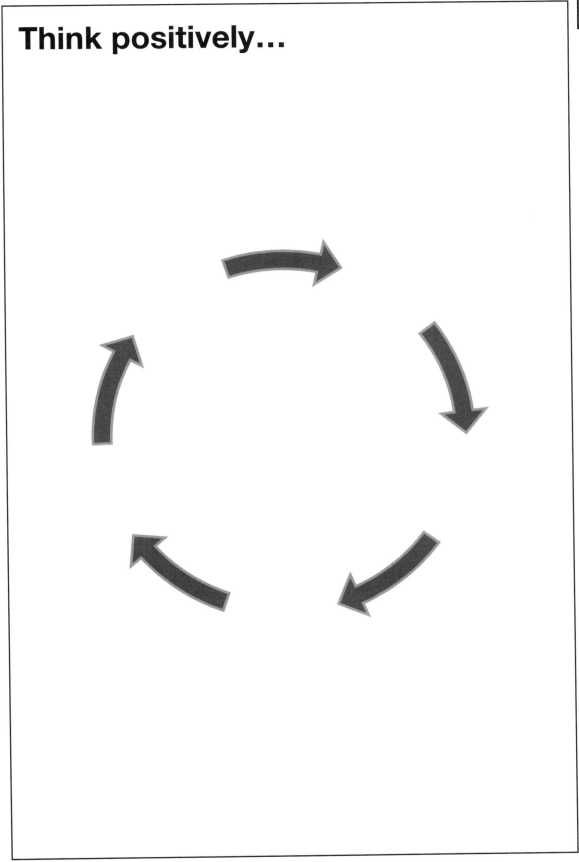

Appendix 2.9

Chapter 3
Body image and appearance

- Flip chart for group rules
- Printed copies of the thought storming activity sheet (enough for one each)
- Picture cards printed, cut out and laminated
- Printed copies of the 'Barbie' activity sheet (at least enough for one between two)
- Barbie images printed, cut out and laminated
- Printed copies of the 'Beyond appearance' activity sheet (enough for one each)
- Copy of the progressive muscle relaxation sequence

Having a positive body image is an important part of emotional well being and good self-esteem. However, around half of girls and a third of boys have dieted to lose weight, and cosmetic surgery rates have increased by nearly 20 per cent since 2008. This lack of body confidence can lead to other social and health problems such as depression, eating disorders and disengagement in learning.

WHAT LEADS TO POOR BODY CONFIDENCE?

The development of a person's own body image is complex and thought to be the product of a range of factors, including family and peer dynamics, the media, cultural and political expectations, as well as personality and experiences. A 2007 report by the American Psychological Association (APA) found that a culture-wide sexualisation of girls (and women) was contributing to increased female anxiety associated with body image. This sexualisation is evident in the portrayal of women in a range of media, such as television programmes and films, music videos and lyrics, toys (e.g. Bratz dolls) and clothing, as well as magazines that are aimed at teenagers but may be dominated by articles on how to look attractive and sexy for men.

RESEARCH AND FINDINGS

An all-party parliamentary group was established in May 2011 and launched an enquiry into the causes and consequences of body image. The enquiry ran from November 2011 to February 2012 and consisted of an online consultation that was open to submissions from the general public, as well as ten oral evidence sessions. Some of the key findings of the enquiry were as follows:

- Parents were one of the main influences on children, and their own body image concerns were mimicked by their children.

- In secondary schools the peer group was the major influence; body dissatisfaction could impact on peer relationships.
- There is a need to equip children, young people and important 'gatekeepers', such as parents and teachers, with the tools to deal with social and cultural pressures to conform to unrealistic beauty ideals.
- The culture of media, advertising and celebrity was perceived to be the main social influence on body image.
- A major contributor to body dissatisfaction was image manipulation and a lack of body diversity in advertising.

Concern over appearance and body shape is not a new phenomenon. Throughout history there have been different standards of what is or is not beautiful and different ways of achieving this ideal. Women in the nineteenth century wore corsets that would cause respiratory problems, and now we try to diet or exercise ourselves into shape. The spread of media has, however, brought obsessions with body image into all aspects of our lives. We are presented with a 'beauty ideal' that lacks diversity and is based on standards that would be impossible to achieve by the majority of the population, but we compare ourselves to these rather than our own family or those with 'normal' good looks.

In this session the main objective is to engage the students in thinking about how they feel about their own images and the effect of the media and celebrity culture on their levels of confidence and self-image. How do they perceive themselves and are these realistic perceptions? Is it right to compare themselves to the idealised and airbrushed images they see in the media?

Group rules

At the beginning of each session the group rules should be revisited. The students should be asked if they wish to make any alterations or additions to these rules. It is important that students are able to refer to these throughout the session, therefore they should be placed somewhere in the room where they will remain visible for the duration.

Talk time

As the students may not have another opportunity during their school week to get together in an 'all-female' environment this time should be used primarily to 'catch up'. It could also be used to review the previous session and to introduce the topic of this current session.

It may also be helpful to then reflect further on the following questions:

How do we define body image?
What image of ourselves would we like other people to see?
What do we think they see?
Is it wrong to present airbrushed images to girls and, if so, why?
Is there a risk of girls becoming fixated on their appearance?
Do boys have problems with their body image too?

Introduction

The issues of body image and appearance could be introduced by way of a thought storming activity using the format provided **(Appendix 3.1)**. Students could be asked to jot down any initial thoughts and ideas about the two terms. This provides the facilitators with an opportunity both to assess the levels of prior knowledge relating to these concepts and to field any questions and clarify new concepts or definitions. It is hoped that each student will have something to contribute. Even those who might struggle here will hopefully have heard something during the talk time which they can jot down.

Icebreaker

This icebreaker activity requires the students to consider a range of images taken from the media. The picture cards shown in **Appendix 3.2** could be spread out over the table in front of the students. Students can then undertake the following activities:

Note down some words that come to mind when you see these images (e.g. wife, mother, age, ageing, ethnicity, weight, sexualised)

Identify where the sexualisation of women occurs and provide examples – music videos, TV, films, magazines, newspapers (No More Page 3 campaign), coverage of sporting events (Fair Game – women in sport campaign), video games

Then consider these facts and discuss what the implications might be for the well being of girls and young women:

We see these images more than we see our own family members.

The current media ideal of thinness for women is achievable by less than 5 per cent of the female population.

Of the images of women we are presented with, 50 per cent have a BMI that is unhealthy (i.e. not enough body fat).

Core activity (a)

This activity uses the 'Barbie' activity sheet **(Appendix 3.3)** and the image shown in **Appendix 3.4**. It is hoped that this activity will help to prompt the students to consider how often media images of women and girls present a very narrow view of what the 'ideal' image is. Students could be presented with the following points:

- We start to recognise ourselves in the mirror from around the age of 2 years of age.
- Girls of 5 years are worried about their weight and appearance.
- Girls only have a couple of years when they don't have these worries.

Facilitators could enable discussion simply by asking the students what they think about these statements. The students could be encouraged to discuss and feedback their ideas. Is this a situation they would wish their own daughters to find themselves in?

The students could then be asked to read through the 'Barbie' activity sheet **(Appendix 3.3)**. It includes statements regarding the unrealistic representation of body size promoted by the Barbie brand and a number of discussion points. In addition the image in **Appendix 3.4** helps illustrate just how unrealistic this representation is. This could be used during the activity alongside the activity sheet.

Core activity (b)

There are far more important things than physical appearance. What we value about our nearest and dearest almost always goes beyond body image and appearance. The 'Beyond appearance' activity sheet **(Appendix 3.5)** encourages the students to think about the talents and achievements of one of their loved ones. The students could be asked to pick somebody they love and to think about what makes them special. What is impressive about them? What are their talents? What are their achievements? What do you value about them?

Target setting

Students could be asked to record in their thought diaries **(Appendix 3.6)** two steps which they could take to help them reach an attainable goal in relation to their appearance. They could ask themselves the following two questions: how do I look now? And, how do I want to look? Students must focus on realistic attainable goals. Discourage them from making comparisons between their own appearance and media images like those used during the icebreaker. For example, most of the women depicted in the print media are way above average in height. It is unrealistic to hope that I will grow another 5 inches, bearing in mind my age and height!

Compliments to close

This section aims to provide each of the students with a positive affirmation. It will be important for the facilitator to ensure that each student is given a compliment either by themselves or by another student member of the group.

There is plenty of anecdotal evidence which suggests that one quick way to boost a woman's opinion of her appearance is compliment her! In this section compliments could focus on body image and appearance. Facilitators could ask the students the following questions:

Whose hair do you like?
Who has good skin?
Who dresses well?
Who appears the most confident about the way they look?

Relaxation

The technique for this session is progressive muscle relaxation, which involves relaxing different parts of the body in a specific sequence, starting at the feet and working up to the face. Facilitators could encourage the students to follow the steps below:

- Get comfortable by loosening clothes, taking off footwear and restrictive jewellery. Lying down on the floor, take a few minutes to relax, breathing in and out in slow, deep breaths.
- When you're relaxed and ready to start, focus your attention to your right foot. Slowly tense the muscles in your right foot, squeezing as tightly as you can. Hold for a count of at least five.
- Relax your right foot focusing on the tension flowing away and the way your foot feels as it becomes loose.
- Stay in this relaxed state for a moment, breathing deeply and slowly.
- When you're ready, shift your attention to your left foot. Follow the same sequence of muscle tension and release.
- Move slowly up through your body, contracting and relaxing the muscle groups as you go.

The most popular sequence runs as follows:

Right foot, left foot, right calf, left calf, right thigh, left thigh, hips and buttocks, stomach, chest, back, right arm and hand, left arm and hand, neck and shoulders, and face.

Additional activities

Airbrushing/spot the difference

It is important that facilitators introduce this activity with a discussion about what is meant by image alteration and digital enhancement. Perhaps the following points could be made:

Almost all media images are manipulated in some way.
There are many different ways in which images can be altered.
Airbrushing technology has advanced to the extent that often images look completely unrealistic, and can represent a degree of perfection which is unattainable.

Once the facilitators feel confident that the students understand the concept, the image in **Appendix 3.7** can be distributed. Discussions should focus on the following:

What is the difference between the before and after shots?
Why might a celebrity prefer the image on the left to be shown in the press, rather than the image on the right?
Why might celebrities want images of themselves to be airbrushed? What do they do? Will looking more attractive help their career?

It is important to note that Britney Spears chose to distribute both the pre- and post-production images of a photo shoot to highlight the extent to which the photos were manipulated. Keira Knightley has also spoken out about the amount of airbrushing that photos of her have undergone.

> *OK, I'm on the cover of a magazine but somebody else does the hair, and the make-up, and airbrushes the f*** out of me – it's not me, it's something other people have created.*

X-treme problems!

This activity sheet **(Appendix 3.8)** features a problem scenario in which a young girl is experiencing body image issues. The students could be asked to consider what advice they might give to the 'writer'. They could also consider ways in which the writer might address this issue. Could they try to focus on something else instead? How might they think about their own body and the bodies of others differently?

As before, this activity could be entirely verbal. If students are reluctant to write their own responses on the activity sheets provided then one of the facilitators could record key themes and ideas which come out of a group discussion on the format provided **(Appendix 3.9)**. The key aim is to encourage students to articulate thoughts and feelings; it does not matter whether this articulation is written or verbal.

Thought storming

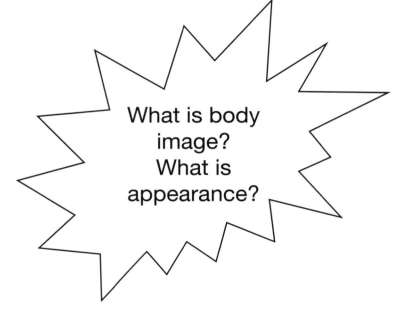

What is body
image?
What is
appearance?

Appendix 3.1

Appendix 3.2a
Sexualised or not?

Appendix 3.2b
Sexualised or not?

There are two Barbie dolls sold every second in the world.

The target market for Barbie sales is young girls aged 3–12.

Slumber Party Barbie was introduced in 1965 and came with a bathroom scale permanently set at 110 lbs with a book entitled *'How to Lose Weight'* with directions inside stating simply 'Don't eat.'

What if Barbie was a real woman???

She would be 5'9" tall, have a 39" bust, an 18" waist, 33" hips and size 3 feet!

At 5'9" tall and weighing 110 lbs. Barbie would have a BMI of 16.24 and fit the weight criteria for anorexia. She would likely not menstruate.
If Barbie was a real woman, she'd have to walk on all fours due to her proportions.

Discuss these points!!!

Is there a fixation with being size zero?

How might having played with such dolls have affected girl's self-image?

What are the physical symptoms of being so underweight?

What do you think now?

Appendix 3.3 All about Barbie

Appendix 3.4 Barbie's proportions

Beyond appearance

Write the name of somebody you love on the trophy below. Try to focus on what impresses you about them. What are their talents? What are their achievements? What do you value about them? Write any ideas in the area surrounding the trophy.

Appendix 3.5 Beyond appearance

My thoughts

	Weekly target
F	
U	
F	

Appendix 3.6 Beyond appearance

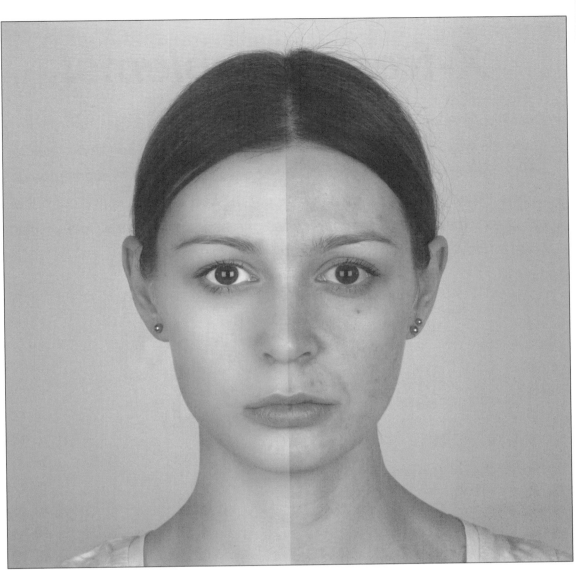

Appendix 3.7 Airbrushing/spot the difference

X-treme problems!

Dear Agony Aunt,

I hate the way I look. I try every week to get out of PE just so I don't have to get undressed in front of people. I've got a wobbly tummy, a fat arse and no boobs. I keep a secret photo album under my bed of pictures I've cut out of my sister's magazines. I look at pictures of Rihanna and Cheryl Cole wishing I had a body like theirs. What's the point if I look this fat? X

Appendix 3.8

Dear Reader,

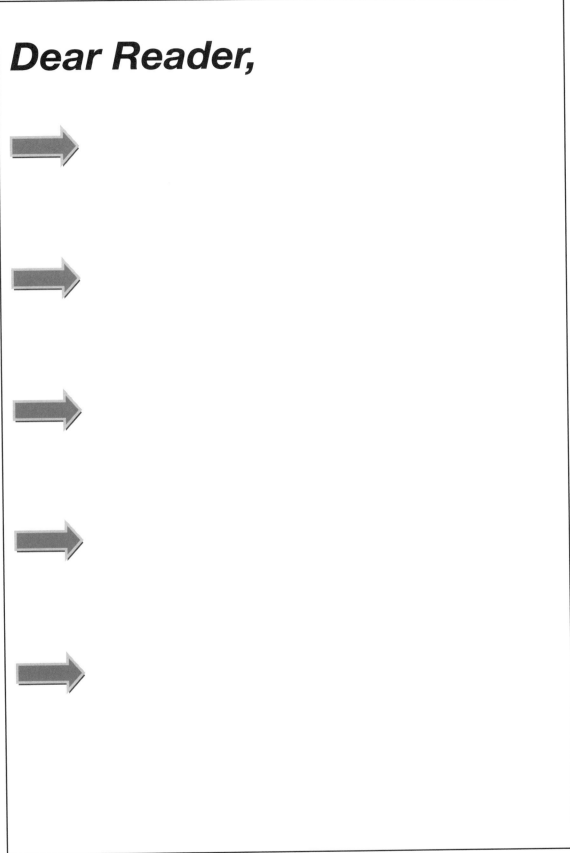

Appendix 3.9

Chapter 4
Stereotypes

A *stereotype* is '. . . a fixed, over generalized belief about a particular group or class of people' (Cardwell, 1996). For example, a 'teenage yob' dressed in a hoodie.

One *advantage* of a stereotype is that it enables us to respond rapidly to situations because we may have had a similar experience before.

One *disadvantage* is that it makes us ignore differences between individuals; therefore we think things about people that might not be true (i.e. make generalisations).

The use of stereotypes is a major way by which we simplify our social world, since they reduce the amount of processing we have to do when we meet a new person. By stereotyping we infer that a person has a whole range of characteristics and abilities that we assume all members of that group have. Stereotypes lead to social categorisation, which is one of the reasons for prejudice attitudes (i.e. 'them' and 'us' mentality) which lead to in-groups and out-groups.

Most stereotypes probably tend to convey a negative impression. Positive examples would include judges (the phrase 'sober as a judge' would suggest this is a stereotype with a very respectable set of characteristics), overweight people (who are often seen as 'jolly') and television newsreaders (usually seen as highly dependable, respectable and impartial). Negative stereotypes seem far more common, however.

RACIAL STEREOTYPES

Researchers have found that stereotypes exist of different races, cultures or ethnic groups. Although the terms race, culture and ethnic groups have different meanings, we shall take them to mean roughly the same thing at the moment.

The most famous study of racial stereotyping was published by Katz and Braly in 1933 when they reported the results of a questionnaire completed by students at Princeton University in the USA. They found that students held clear, negative stereotypes – few students expressed any difficulty in responding to the questionnaire.

Most students at that time would have been white Americans, and the perceptions of other ethnic groups included Jews as shrewd and mercenary, Japanese as shrewd and sly, Negroes as lazy and happy-go-lucky and Americans as industrious and intelligent.

Not surprisingly, racial stereotypes always seem to favour the race of the holder and belittle other races. It is probably true to say that every ethnic group has racial stereotypes of other groups; some psychologists argue that it is a 'natural' aspect of human behaviour, which can be seen to benefit each group because it helps in the long run to identify with one's own ethnic group and so find protection and promote the safety and success of the group. There is no evidence for this view, however, and many writers argue that it is merely a way of justifying racist attitudes and behaviours.

Group rules

At the beginning of each session the group rules should be revisited. The students should be asked if they wish to make any alterations or additions to these rules. It is important that students are able to refer to these throughout the session, therefore they should be placed somewhere in the room where they will remain visible for the duration.

Talk time

As the students may not have another opportunity during their school week to get together in an 'all-female' environment this time should be used primarily to 'catch up'. It could also be used to review the previous session and to introduce the topic of this current session. The facilitator could initially pose the question: What is a stereotype? A thought storming activity sheet has been provided **(Appendix 4.1)**.

Icebreaker

Using a round-table format each member of the group could identify their favourite item of clothing along with an explanation of why it is so special to them. Here students are learning something quite neutral about each other. Exchanges like this help to start to build a safe and trusting group environment.

Introduction

For this activity each student should be provided with the 'Stereotypical teens?' thought storming activity sheet **(Appendix 4.2)**. Students could be asked to think of as many stereotypical statements they can think which refer to young people. Some examples could be 'all teenage mums are sluts' and 'teenage boys don't wash'.

Students are next asked to reflect upon the fact that many young people frequently feel rejected or isolated from older people in their community. This can sometimes be seen as the result of a lack of communication between the generations and also a certain level of stereotyping undertaken on both sides. This kind of stereotyping and the way in which young people are sometimes perceived by the older generation can ultimately cause damaging levels of fear and lead to the demonisation of young people, often without justification.

The idea of this session is to highlight strengths and positive qualities that young people bring to their communities and to also reinforce the fact that it's possible to change other people's views and opinions, particularly when our actions are positive and achieve positive results within our local community.

The students can be asked to focus on the following questions:

- For many young people negative or antisocial behaviour is the direct result of the fact that there is no available outlet for them in their local communities. Do you agree with this?
- Is there a local youth centre in your area?
- Is there an appropriate level of support for young people?
- Are there things for teenagers to do where you live? If not, what do they need in terms of provision?
- What suggestions would you make to those in power in your local community?

Facilitators could record any key themes or ideas that come out of this discussion either onto a flip chart or a whiteboard.

Core activity (a)

One of the labels often given to teenagers is that they are 'feckless' particularly in relation to sexual activity and having babies very early in their lives. For many older people being a teenage mum has extremely negative connotations. For example, teenage mums are frequently presented as 'benefit scroungers' and 'as getting pregnant in order to gain social housing', mainly at the cost of more traditional families who apparently cannot access such support.

It's important throughout this activity to discuss possible reasons for young girls wanting to have babies at a very early age and highlight that often this occurs due to lack of education and knowledge of conception and contraception. In no sense should there be a focus on condemning such young people, but rather the focus needs to be on identifying risk factors and also what young people need should they become a teenage mum.

The students can debate the following statements in turn:

- Young girls get pregnant so that they can get benefits.
- Young girls get pregnant because they are damaged and lonely and want someone of their own to love.
- Pregnant teens get too much help.
- Teenage mums should give up their children for adoption because they cannot give them a good enough life.
- Being a teenage mum puts enormous stress on relationships and also on the well being of the individuals concerned.

Core activity (b)

The students could be asked to read through *The Guardian* article titled 'It seems that we can only be interesting if we are smoking, snorting or stabbing'. The article can be found using the following link (www.guardian.co.uk/society/2009/apr/15/stereotypes-young-people).

Students could then be asked to discuss these experiences along with their own and consider what needs to change in order to address these stereotypes. What can they do? What can others do? What would make a difference and change people's behaviours and perceptions?

Reflections and feedback

The students should be given the opportunity to offer any feedback they may have regarding this session. Facilitators could also encourage students to reflect on the learning that has taken place, using the following conversation prompts:

What is a stereotype?
Have you ever been stereotyped?
How did this make you feel?
Have you ever made a snap judgement about somebody?
Have you come across a stereotype during this session which you didn't recognise as a stereotype before?

Target setting

The students could be asked to keep an eye out for stereotypical representations in the media. If they recognise any they could make a note of it in their thought diaries ready for a discussion in the next session.

Compliments to close

This section aims to provide each of the students with a positive affirmation. It will be important for the facilitator to ensure that each student is given a compliment either by themselves or by another student member of the group. To facilitate engagement with this, facilitators could offer prompts such as:

Name one aspect of this session which you enjoyed.
Name one aspect of this session which you have found useful.
Whose company have you really enjoyed this week?
Whose company do you feel you have benefited from?

Relaxation

The relaxation for this week is a nature scavenger hunt activity. This involves the students walking around outdoors, searching for the items specified on the 'Nature scavenger hunt' activity sheet **(Appendix 4.3)**. Most of the items can be found on school grounds so there is no need for the students to stray far. The students are asked to leave the items where they find them, not to collect them as they go. The intended outcome here is that students will relax whilst being outdoors. They may also find focusing on something quite neutral relaxing after a full session.

Additional activities

Cookie cutter kid

This activity uses the activity sheet in **Appendix 4.4**. Students could be asked to draw an image of a stereotypical 'teenage mum' or a stereotypical 'layabout lad' using the gingerbread man shape as a base. Facilitators should engage students in discussions about what they have chosen to draw and why. For example, if they have chosen to dress their 'layabout lad' in a hoodie they should be asked why they have chosen to do this and whether or not they recognise this as a stereotype.

Snap judgements

This activity requires the stereotype cards to be printed, cut out and laminated **(Appendix 4.5)**. These could be spread out over the table in front of the students. They could then be asked to match up any pairs they recognise as stereotypes. They should be made aware that some of the cards may have more than one 'partner'.

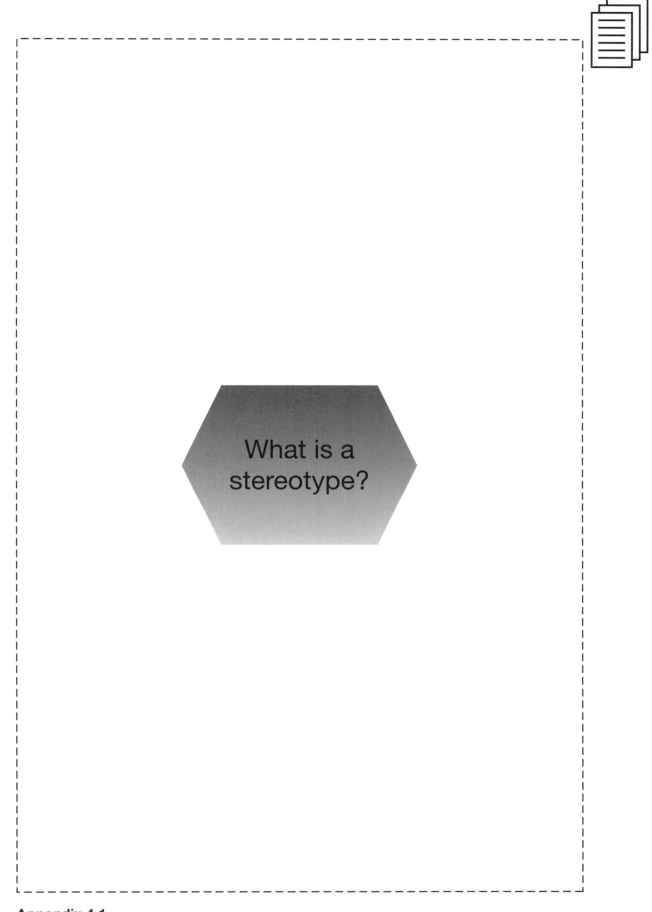

What is a
stereotype?

Appendix 4.1

Stereotypical teens?

Appendix 4.2 Stereotypical teens?

Nature scavenger hunt

Try to find the items listed below but do not collect them!

Only check off the items you see. Please leave the items where you find them to avoid disturbing wildlife.

Something round

Something scented

Something green

Something that can be tied

Something rough

Something thin

Something with veins

Something opaque

Something brittle

Something that looks like a 'Y'

Appendix 4.3

Appendix 4.4 Cookie cutter kid

Pop Star	Men	Person on Benefits
Anti-Social Behaviour	'Well Endowed'	Good Dancer
Scottish	Cocaine User	Teenage Boy
French	Model	Heavy Drinker
Black	Onions	Aggressive
Smelly	American	Women
Anti-Social Behaviour	'Chav'	Sleeps Around
Logical	Welsh	Goes out without a coat
Has Sex with sheep	Smells of Curry	Emotional
Housework	Irish	Fat
Owns a Corner Shop	Tracksuit	Sullen
Indian	Lazy	Scrounger
Northern	Eating Disorder	Competitive

Appendix 4.5

Chapter 5
Relationships part 1

Resources required

- Flip chart for group rules
- Desired activity sheets
- Response cards, printed and laminated
- Scenario cards, printed and laminated

Group rules

At the beginning of each session the group rules should be revisited. The students should be asked if they wish to make any alterations or additions to these rules. It is important that students are able to refer to these throughout the session, therefore they should be placed somewhere in the room where they will remain visible for the duration.

Talk time

As the students don't have another opportunity during their school week to get together in an 'all-female' environment this time should be used primarily to 'catch up'. It could also be used to review the previous session and to introduce the topic of this current session.

The students could be asked to complete the 'Relationship rating' activity sheet in **Appendix 5.1**. Here, the students are asked to identify five relationships they have currently. These could be with family members, with teachers, with professionals or with friends. For each relationship, students should indicate a 'relationship rating' score by colouring in the smiley faces. This will help the facilitators gain an insight into which relationships are treasured most by the students. It also provides the students with the opportunity to recognise just how many relationships they are part of.

N.B. Students do not have to name individuals. For example, if they prefer they could write 'teacher' in the relationship column as opposed to 'Miss Piggott'.

Introduction

In order to introduce the topic facilitators could ask students to complete the following sentences:

'A relationship is . . .'
'Relationships are . . .'

Students could either focus on defining the term (e.g. 'a relationship is a connection between two people') or on the benefits of being in relationships (e.g. relationships are satisfying). This could follow a round-table format with the students taking it in turns to complete one or both of the sentences.

Icebreaker

Each student should be given a copy of the 'Work the room' activity sheet in **Appendix 5.2**. The students are given a number of small tasks including:

How many green eyes are there in the room?
Who has made the longest journey into school?
Who has the most unusual hobby?

Students should be encouraged to ask each other the relevant questions whilst moving around the room. This activity encourages students to talk to other group members who they might not talk to as much outside of these sessions. Each student must speak with everyone else in order to answer the questions above. This is particularly pertinent if most of the session is conducted with the students sitting round a large table so that mostly they speak to those either on their right or on their left.

The activity sheet also asks the students to identify five different phobias. The answers are as follows:

Hippopotomonstrosesquippedaliophobia – fear of long words
Arachibutyrophobia – fear of peanut butter sticking to the roof of the mouth
Alektorophobia – fear of chickens
Ephebiphobia – fear of teenagers
Anglophobia – fear of England or English culture.

Core activity (a)

It is important that students understand the term 'relational aggression' and how these kinds of insidious bullying behaviours can impact negatively upon the development and maintenance of healthy relationships. Aggression is generally defined as a behaviour that's intended to harm others. It can take many forms, but physical forms of aggression – getting into physical fights, dating violence or violent crimes – have received the most attention from researchers, educators and parents. Such people are understandably interested in protecting their children from the serious harm that physical aggression often inflicts.

Many studies also show that relational and other non-physical forms of aggression are just as harmful to an individual's ability to learn, grow and succeed. Relational aggression encompasses behaviours that harm others by damaging, threatening to damage or manipulating their relationships with their peers, or by injuring their feelings of social acceptance.

Some examples of such behaviours can be provided for the students including:

- Giving someone the silent treatment and ignoring them
- Spreading rumours and stories about someone
- Telling others not to go around with someone as a means of retaliation

The students are encouraged to consider what other kinds of relational aggression they have observed or are aware of, and to think particularly about the consequences for both the victims and the perpetrators. Many young people who have been on the receiving end of such relational aggression have become school-refusers, engaged in self-harming behaviours and, in a significant minority of cases, have committed suicide. The students themselves may be aware of more recent instances of young people committing suicide as a result of such aggression and bullying.

It may also be useful to consider how such behaviours can be tackled within the school context and to ask the students to answer the following questions:

- What can the students and staff do to reduce instances of relational aggression and also to raise awareness among young people as to how and why this behaviour occurs?
- What can they do in terms of the way they behave and in the way the school systems are set up in order to reduce such behaviours?

Once again this is a sensitive issue and the facilitator needs to be aware of this fact, and to also be careful not to engage with students in revealing the identity of any of their peers who may be engaging in this kind of aggressive behaviour. The rule of 'no names' needs to be reinforced. The students should not be naming anyone who is bullying or upsetting others. What they need to do is ensure that they feed this information back to the appropriate member of staff so that the school's anti-bullying procedures can be adhered to. The facilitator needs to reinforce this throughout this activity alongside the fact that overall the aim here is to ensure that the students not only recognise relational aggression but also begin to think how they can respond to it in a more positive and powerful manner.

Core activity (b)

This role play activity focuses on how to respond to the types of relational aggression that were explored during the previous activity. It requires both the 'Response' cards **(Appendix 5.3)** and the 'Scenario' cards **(Appendix 5.4)** to be both printed and laminated prior to the session.

The students should be organised into three groups so that each group is able to select one of the scenario cards. The members of that group should then decide who will play the bystanders, who will play the 'victim', and who will play the 'aggressors'. The 'victim' should then come forward to select one of the response cards. These should be placed face down on a table so that the aggressors/bystanders cannot see which card has been selected. After the role play it is up to the aggressors and bystanders to decide whether their 'victim' was responding to them in an aggressive, passive or assertive manner. Each approach should then be discussed with the group.

Facilitators should stress that an assertive response involves describing your feelings and thoughts directly to another person in an honest and appropriate way that respects both you and the other person. It enables you to stand up for yourself and to express honest feelings comfortably, and to exercise personal rights without denying the rights of others.

An aggressive response would involve expressing your feelings indirectly through insults, aggressive statements and aggressive actions. Aggressive responses often involve expressing thoughts and feelings in a way that violates others' rights to be treated with respect and dignity.

A passive response involves saying nothing in reaction to this aggression. Those who respond passively may keep their feelings to themselves; they may hide their feelings from others, and perhaps even hide their feelings from themselves.

Reflections and feedback

The students should be given the opportunity to offer any feedback they may have regarding this session. Facilitators could also encourage students to reflect on the learning that has taken place using the following conversation prompts:

- How did you feel at the start of this session?
- Do you feel any different now?
- Is there anything we did today that you would like more of?
- Is there anything we did today that you would like less of?

Target setting

The students could be asked to record any friendly acts they perform for others, or any friendly acts that others perform for them during the week in their thought diaries.

Compliments to close

This section aims to provide each of the students with a positive affirmation. It will be important for the facilitator to ensure that each student is given a compliment either by themselves or by another student member of the group.

To encourage engagement with this, facilitators could offer prompts such as:

- Name one aspect of this session which you have enjoyed.
- Name one aspect of this session which you have found useful.

During this session students could also be asked to identify 'what makes them a good friend'. They could be asked to write down a couple of key points on Post-it notes to be stuck on their picture portraits. It is hoped that students will at this stage feel confident in complimenting themselves. If this is not the case perhaps other members of the group could offer their own suggestions.

Relaxation

Students could be offered this opportunity to practise some relaxed breathing. This is best done in a quiet place where you are unlikely to be disturbed. Students could be asked to follow the steps below:

- Loosen or remove any tight clothes you have on, such as shoes or jackets. Make yourself feel completely comfortable.

- Lying on the floor, place your arms a little bit away from the side of your body with the palms up. Stretch out your legs, keeping them hip-width apart or slightly wider.
- Breathe in and out slowly and in a regular rhythm as this will help you to calm down.
- Fill up the whole of your lungs with air, without forcing. Imagine you're filling up a bottle, so that your lungs fill from the bottom.
- Breathe in through your nose and out through your mouth.
- Breathe in slowly and regularly counting from one to five (don't worry if you can't reach five at first).
- Then let the breath escape slowly, counting from one to five.
- Keep doing this until you feel calm.

Additional activities

W.L.T.M.

This activity involves the students drafting their own personal advertisement. Students should include in their adverts the characteristics that mean the most to them when thinking about friendship. An example could be:

Sixteen-year-old female seeking new best friend! Must be caring, trusting and must always have my back! Must also love *Hollyoaks*, shopping and food! Drug users need not apply!

If a longer activity is required students could be asked to draft a 'job advert' for a new friend including 'essential' and 'desirable' requirements.

Top tips

Students could be asked to brainstorm a list of 'top tips' for 'how to be a good friend' using the format provided **(Appendix 5.5)**. This could be kept visible so that it can be periodically discussed and new rules can be added if needed.

Relationship Rating

Relationship	Happy	Happier		Happiest
	☺ ☺ ☺ ☺ ☺			
	☺ ☺ ☺ ☺ ☺			
	☺ ☺ ☺ ☺ ☺			
	☺ ☺ ☺ ☺ ☺			
	☺ ☺ ☺ ☺ ☺			

Appendix 5.1

Work the room

How many green eyes are there in the room?

Who has made the longest journey into school?

Who has the most unusual hobby?

What is the weirdest thing anyone has ever eaten?

Who has had the most embarrassing experience?

Who has the most siblings?

Who has the most number of pets?

How many left-handed people are there in the room?

Who is the oldest in the room?

Who knows what 'Hippopotomonstrosesquippedaliophobia' is a fear of? If that's too easy you can try Arachibutyrophobia, Alektorophobia, Ephebiphobia or Anglophobia.

Work it! work it!

Appendix 5.2

ASSERTIVE

PASSIVE

AGGRESSIVE

Appendix 5.3

Scenario 1

You're making your way to the next lesson through the crowded hallway. Another female student bumps into you. This causes you to drop your bag on the floor and stuff goes everywhere, including a tampon without its wrapper. Other students walk around the mess but the female student stops as she exclaims 'urgh that's rank! You fucking tramp!' Her friends join in pointing and laughing.

Scenario 2

You're having lunch with some friends. One of your friends points to another female student sitting at the table across from you. She starts whispering insults about the girl to your group. Your friends start laughing out loud. You know that the girl must be able to tell that your table is talking about her. Encouraged by her friends' laughter she throws another insult louder this time. Again, her friends laugh.

Scenario 3

You're getting changed for PE with the rest of the female students. For a laugh you decide to run around snapping the bra straps of the other girls. You go to snap the strap of one student when you realise she's not wearing a bra. You point saying 'you've got no boobs! Why don't you go get changed with the boys?'. Your friends laugh along with you.

Appendix 5.4

Top tips for 'good friends'

Appendix 5.5

Chapter 6
Relationships part 2

- Flip chart for group rules
- Desired activity sheets
- Behaviour cards, printed and laminated
- Statement cards, printed and laminated
- Ready-made cupcakes, icing and decorations
- Laptops with internet access
- Blindfolds or scarves

In this session students are introduced to the concept of healthy romantic/sexual relationships. It's important at the beginning of the session to focus on the fact that there is a clear distinction between healthy and unhealthy relationships. Those that are healthy will tend to promote and ensure the well being of the people involved in the relationship.

A key element of this session is to reinforce the fact that students need to be very careful about entering into any form of relationship which is remotely abusive. If they begin to consider that abusive relationships fall within the framework of 'normal', then they will be at greater risk of developing mental ill-health in the longer term. They will also be engaging in unsafe behaviours and putting themselves and others at risk.

People who tolerate others who hurt or abuse them, either emotionally or physically, are always at risk of developing or experiencing mental health issues. This is something that needs to be reinforced at the outset, particularly given the increasing prevalence of young teenage girls and boys in relationships who consider that physical and sexual abuse are normal within such relationships.

This is a sensitive issue and particularly pertinent at the current time given recent press reports and research into the ways in which teenagers enter into abusive relationships, particularly when they are involved in gang culture. It is important that facilitators reassure the students that they can and should be free to talk about such issues in a sensitive and empathic way with each other. It is when these kinds of concerns are covered up and not discussed that abuse can take place and be maintained over long periods of time. The students may well be aware of instances such as the Bradford girls who were abused over time in their relationships with a group of Asian men. Unfortunately, some people may well think that these girls engaged in consensual sex. It is important to note that this was certainly not the case in this particular situation, and what the facilitator should be emphasising throughout this session is that any relationship that is dominated by non-consensual sex cannot be perceived to be a healthy relationship in any sense. It is important to emphasise the fact that the contents of this session are clearly aiming to support students in remaining both healthy and safe in their interactions with others, particularly when these relationships involve the expression of physical love and desire.

Group rules

At the beginning of each session the group rules should be revisited. The students should be asked if they wish to make any alterations or additions to these rules. It is important that students are able to refer to these throughout the session, therefore they should be placed somewhere in the room where they will remain visible for the duration.

It is vital that the facilitator is sensitive towards and aware of students who may have witnessed such unhealthy relationships or be living in homes where such relationships are ongoing and visible to them. It is vital to reinforce the fact that students do not need to discuss or reveal any information that is of a sensitive nature that would make them feel uncomfortable in this context. However, the facilitator needs to also reinforce the fact that should anyone become upset or concerned about anything or feel the need to talk further about something in their own lives or a relationship that is worrying them in their own families then they need to do so at the end of the session. Support systems in the school should be available to students to ensure that there is someone that they can talk to in confidence (in line with child protection procedures) in order to address any of these concerns or issues.

It's also important to encourage young people to discuss such issues and not to try to cover up these kinds of problems or difficulties. There are a range of agencies where young people can obtain help and it's important to provide an opportunity for the young people themselves to identify such agencies within their own local context.

Talk time

As the students may not have another opportunity during their school week to get together in an 'all-female' environment this time should be used primarily to 'catch up'. It could also be used to review the previous session and to introduce the topic of this current session.

The main focus of this talk time is to discuss responses to the key question:

What is a healthy romantic relationship?

In this discussion activity the students are asked to work as a whole group to answer the question provided. It's important to encourage students to articulate their views here, particularly when defining the nature of a healthy relationship. This is clearly one in which both human beings feel safe and secure and able to nurture and support each other. A format has been provided for this to allow either the facilitator or the students to make notes of key ideas and themes **(Appendix 6.1)**.

The facilitator may wish to highlight some key pieces of information for the students here. Unhealthy relationships are those in which one person tends to dominate the other, either physically, emotionally or mentally, and in which the dominated person begins to take on the role of the victim. It's also important to raise the issue of victims within such relationships and to consider why they may stay in such an unhealthy partnership. This may include reference to issues of low self-esteem and the need to feel valued. It's evident that many young people in abusive relationships stay in such relationships due to the fact that they have low levels of self-esteem and confidence and feel that they are, in effect, lucky to have any form of relationship with a member of their peer group.

Introduction

This activity is intended to introduce the issue of abuse within romantic and sexual relationships. The 'talk time' activity focused on the positive attributes of a healthy relationship, whereas the introduction activity begins to explore those relationships that aren't healthy, and that do not promote and ensure the well being of the people involved.

This activity requires the behaviour cards **(Appendix 6.2)** to be printed, separated and laminated prior to the session. These can then be handed to the students so that they can sort them according to the type of behaviour represented – 'Abusive', 'Supportive' or 'Depends'.

Facilitators could encourage discussion by offering the following conversation prompts:

How does an apparently supportive behaviour become an abusive one?
What would a relationship be like if it involved the abusive group of behaviours?
Who would feel good/bad?
Who would have the power/no power?
Would the relationship be equal and fair?

Facilitators could also help the students explore those behaviours that they placed in the 'Depends' group by asking the following:

What does it depend on?
Is it about how much or how often?
Is it the way that it is done?
Is it the reason behind the behaviour?
Is it about both parties being in agreement?

Icebreaker

This activity involves the students sharing facts about themselves with the other group members. The number of facts they are required to share depends on how much toilet paper they take. The facilitator should begin by instructing the students to take as much toilet paper as they would use for a visit to the toilet from the roll of toilet paper provided. Once all the students have done so the facilitator should start by tearing off one sheet of their paper, scrunching it up and throwing it into the middle of the table whilst sharing a fact about themselves. The facts do not have to be personal or sensitive; perhaps to demonstrate this, the facilitator could begin with disclosing their shoe size. The activity continues in this manner until everybody has used up their paper.

Core activity (a)

This activity involves the statement cards in **Appendix 6.3**. The statements represent various beliefs about the different roles etc. that men and women may play in romantic relationships. These cards should be printed, separated and laminated before the start of this session, as they will also be needed for the second core activity.

This activity requires facilitators to identify a continuum line, from strongly agree to strongly disagree, perhaps by sticking up the cards in **Appendix 6.4** on opposing walls. The students could then be asked to place themselves along this line in response to the statements being read out. The facilitators should ask students to explain their position. They could also prompt further discussion by posing the following:

Would your position be the same if we were to change the gender involved? For example, if you agree that men should open doors for women, do you believe that it is wrong for a women to hold a door open for a man?

If you don't agree, where do you think the idea came from?

What impact do you think this statement has on both women and men and the romantic relationships they have?

What if two people didn't agree on this statement but were in a relationship together? Would this cause tension?

Core activity (b)

For this activity the students should be asked to sort themselves into small groups. Each group could then be asked to pick one statement card they would like to debate. The group should then decide which student/students will argue the 'agree' position and which will argue the 'disagree' position. Students should be allowed some time with which to formulate their ideas before sharing them with the opposing team. Facilitators could prompt further thinking by asking students whether or not they see any of the statements differently after exploring and discussing them.

Reflections and feedback

The students should be given the opportunity to offer any feedback they may have regarding this session. Facilitators could also encourage students to reflect on the learning that has taken place, using the following conversation prompts:

How did you feel at the start of this session?

Do you feel any different now?

Is there anything we did today that you would like more of?

Is there anything we did today that you would like less of?

Identify one thing you have learnt during this session.

This reflection time also provides an opportunity for the facilitators to remind the students about the support systems in the school that are available to them. Perhaps facilitators could conclude by reaffirming the following key messages:

Nobody ever deserves to be abused.

There are sources of help that are available to you, some within the school.

Domestic and sexual abuse is unacceptable and in many cases criminal. The police take it seriously and have specially trained officers to respond to domestic abuse.

Target setting

The students could be asked to share one thing that they have learnt during this session with somebody outside of the group. Perhaps facilitators could reinforce the importance of talking about these issues and the notion that silence can help abuse to take place over long periods of time.

Compliments to close

This section aims to provide each of the students with a positive affirmation. It will be important for the facilitator to ensure that each student is given a compliment either by themselves or by another student member of the group.

Students could be asked to offer the person to their right a compliment, based on either their credentials as a friend or as a group member. This helps reinforce learning which took place in the previous session which focused on different forms of relationships including friendships.

Relaxation

The relaxation activity for this session could be cupcake decorating. Students would need to be provided with a number of ready-made cupcakes (shop bought or home-made), a selection of decorations and some ready-made icing. It is hoped that students will find this sort of creativity relaxing and that this will help them 'draw a line' under the session.

Additional activities

X-treme problems!

This activity sheet **(Appendix 6.5)** features a problem scenario in which a teenage girl is involved in an unhealthy and abusive relationship. The students could be asked to consider what advice they might give to the 'writer'. They could also consider ways in which the writer might address this issue.

This activity could be entirely verbal. If students are reluctant to write their own responses then one of the facilitators could record key themes and ideas which come out of a group discussion. The key aim is to encourage students to articulate thoughts and feelings; it does not matter whether this articulation is written or verbal.

Spread the news

Students could be asked to draft a public awareness campaign highlighting the issue of abuse within teenage relationships. This could include a print advertisement, a 30- or 60-second radio advertisement or a printed leaflet.

Students should be provided with laptops so that the can gather information to include in their campaigns. Facilitators could direct students to the following websites:

www.womensaid.org.uk
www.nationaldomesticviolencehelpline.org.uk
www.homeoffice.gov.uk/crime/violence-against-women-girls/teenage-relationship-abuse
http://thisisabuse.direct.gov.uk/

Blind cat and mouse

This trust game is intended to highlight how uncomfortable it can be putting your trust in someone and how important communication is within a relationship.

The students should be placed in groups of four. Student one is selected to be the mouse, student two is selected to be the cat, student three is selected to be the mouse trainer and student four is selected to be the cat trainer. Both the cat and mouse are blindfolded so that they must rely on their trainers to direct them. This can be done by agreeing signals such as patting, clapping hands or snapping fingers. These directions should be agreed on before the start of play (for example, left could be 1x pat and right could be 2x pat. Go could be a hand clap and stop could be a finger snap). The game begins with the cat and mouse at opposite ends of the room with their trainers standing behind them. The cat trainer must then direct the cat towards the mouse in order to 'catch' it, whilst the mouse trainer must help the mouse to escape.

It is important the facilitators relate this activity to being in a relationship. They could do so by posing the following questions:

- What was it like to guide and be guided/to trust and be trusted?
- Is it important to trust and be trusted in a relationship?
- How important was clear communication in this game? How does that relate to relationships?
- What does it feel like to be safe with someone?

What is a healthy romantic relationship?

❖

❖

❖

❖

❖

❖

❖

❖

❖

Appendix 6.1

Holding my hand and cuddling me all the time
Telling me I'm loved
Smiling at me
Putting me down, especially in public
Having to do what he/she wants to avoid arguments
Ignoring me when we're with his/her friends
Telling me I am putting on weight
Giving me a hug when I'm upset
Phoning and texting me all the time
Buying me a present after an argument
Telling me I look nice
Turning up to surprise me
Making me feel really special
Treating me as an equal
Making me feel nervous when we are together
Shouting at me when I do things wrong
Sulking when I have a night out with my mates
Questioning what I wear
Asking where I am going or where I have been
Always interrupting and correcting me
Asking me what I want
Expecting me to pay for everything when we are out
Making fun of everything I say
Doing things that he/she doesn't really like just to please me
Getting angry over something small because he/she has been drinking
Cooking my favourite food for me
Looking after me when I am ill
Having pet names for me
Texting me little love messages all the time

Appendix 6.2

Men should open doors for women
Women should stay at home and look after the children
Men should not talk about their feelings
Women must be slim and attractive if they want to be happy in a relationship
Men should bring in the money to support the family
Women shouldn't bother trying to have careers as they'll only go off and get pregnant after a few years
Men should be able to see their partner or children whenever they like
Women should never make the first move
Men who stay at home and look after the kids aren't real men
If a women gets jealous it must mean she loves her partner
Men are stronger than women
Women need men to look after them
If a man pays for things on a date he can expect the woman to do what he wants
Women should not go out alone at night
Men should know how to fix things
Women should keep a nice home for their family
Men should be the head of the family
It's OK for a man to hurt or threaten his partner if they have been annoyed
If a woman's family tell her to marry someone she should
It's OK for a man to decide where his partner can go and who they can see

Appendix 6.3

STRONLY AGREE

STRONLY DISAGREE

Appendix 6.4

X-treme problems!

Dear Agony Aunt,

I've been dating Tom for 4 months now. He's my brother's mate so when we first started going out all my friends were dead jealous. He's fit, funny and good at sport. Even my mum likes him!

For the first couple of months, I was happy. But I'm starting to miss my friends. I spend so much time with him I barely see anyone else. It's just easier this way. When I do see my friends they just ask me if everything is OK which gets on my nerves.

How do I get things back to how they were?

Appendix 6.5

Chapter 7
Bullying

Resources required

- Flip chart for group rules
- Desired activity sheets
- A large orange and perhaps a stopwatch
- Materials such as A4 white paper (pre-folded as leaflets) and pens/pencils
- Laptops with internet access
- A candle
- Large sheets of paper (A2 or A1)

Bullying is a relationship problem that requires relationship solutions. Bullying is a form of abuse at the hands of peers that can take different forms at different ages and stages of our lives. Bullying is defined as repeated aggression in which there is an imbalance of power between the child who bullies and the child who is victimised (Olweus, 1991; Pepler & Craig, 2000; WriteWork, 2008). Through our research, we understand bullying as a disrespectful relationship problem:

- Children who bully are learning to use power and aggression to control and distress others.
- Children who are victimised become increasingly powerless and find themselves trapped in relationships in which they are being abused.

With repeated bullying, the child who bullies increases in power and the victimised child loses power in the relationship. In such a relationship, children who are being bullied become increasingly powerless to defend themselves. Children who repeatedly bully are establishing unhealthy patterns of behaviour in terms of using power and aggression as a means of relating to others.

Group rules

At the beginning of each session the group rules should be revisited. The students should be asked if they wish to make any alterations or additions to these rules. It is important that students are able to refer to these throughout the session, therefore they should be placed somewhere in the room where they will remain visible for the duration.

Talk time

As the students may not have another opportunity during their school week to get together in an 'all-female' environment this time should be used primarily to 'catch up'.

It could also be used to review the previous session and to introduce the topic of this current session.

The students can initially focus on the question 'what is bullying?' and attempt to make up their own definitions. These can be recorded on a flip chart/electronic whiteboard by the facilitator. Alternatively if the facilitators wish they could make use of the thought storming format provided **(Appendix 7.1)**.

Icebreaker

This game is called 'pass the orange'. Facilitators should ask the students to form a circle. 'Player one' should be passed the large orange. This should be passed around the circle, from one player to the next, using only chin and neck. If at any point the orange is dropped it must be returned to the previous player in the circle to restart the game.

Introduction

The students could be provided with the information sheet (www.youngminds.org.uk/for_children_young_people/whats_worrying_you/bullying/about_bullying) and asked to then create their own illustrated advice booklets for students in their own school ('what to do if . . .'). Use can be made of the internet in order to also highlight available resources and support agencies both locally and nationally and also the current school-based support systems available to young people in the school.

Core activity (a)

Cyberbullying is the use of technology to harass, threaten, embarrass or target another person. It often occurs among young people because of their frequent use of such technology. When an adult is involved, it may meet the definition of cyber-harassment or cyber-stalking, a crime that can have legal consequences and involve jail time.

Sometimes cyberbullying can be easy to spot – for example, if someone's child shows them a text message, tweet or response to a status update on Facebook that is harsh, mean or cruel. Other acts are less obvious, like impersonating a victim online or posting personal information, photos or videos designed to hurt or embarrass another person. Some children and young people report that a fake account, web page or online persona has been created with the sole intention to harass and bully.

Cyberbullying also can happen accidentally. The impersonal nature of text messages, instant messaging and emails make it very hard to detect the sender's tone – one person's joke could be another's hurtful insult. Nevertheless, a repeated pattern of emails, text messages and online posts is rarely accidental.

The students are encouraged to consider the ways in which young people and adults can and do use the internet to bully others.

The list of means of hurting others provided by the Centre for Safe and Responsible Internet Use can be given to the students as follows:

- *Cyber-stalking*
  Harassment that includes threats of harm or is highly intimidating.

- *Denigration (put-downs)*
  Sending or posting harmful, untrue or cruel statements about a person to other people.
- *Exclusion*
  Actions that specifically and intentionally exclude a person from an online group, such as exclusion from an IM 'buddies' list.
- *Flaming*
  Sending angry, rude or vulgar messages directed at a person or persons privately or to an online group.
- *Outing and trickery*
  Sending or posting material about a person that contains sensitive, private or embarrassing information, including forwarding private messages or images. Engaging in tricks to solicit embarrassing information that is then made public.

It may be particularly useful to consider the ways in which older men who are paedophiles masquerade as younger boys in order to groom potential victims. The students can be encouraged to consider how this might be done and what the potential risks might be. These are clearly evident to many people. However, there are always vulnerable young children who will not see such risks and will be genuinely sucked into such an inappropriate relationship over the internet. What is important here is for the facilitator to manage this activity with great sensitivity and also to ensure that it is appropriately boundaried. For example, some students may wish to catastrophise this particular topic and engage in some very graphic and detailed conversations – this is not the idea here. The facilitator can support the activity by again acting as the scribe for the students using a flip chart and recording in bullet points a list of ways in which people can masquerade in order to groom potential victims. The idea here is to then emphasise the importance of ensuring that children and young people do actually become aware of these strategies so that they can act appropriately in order to develop their own well being.

Core activity (b)

Students could be asked to depict a common 'bullying' scenario which they are familiar with using the 'My story board' template **(Appendix 7.2)**. Using the templates should help the students to see how the different scenes of their narrative fit together. Their pictures do not need to be high quality; they just need to act as a guide for the facilitators to see how the scenes will look. If the students wish to they can further clarify what's going on by jotting down a few notes by each picture. An extension of this activity could involve filming each scenario using the group members as the cast.

Reflections and feedback

The students should be given the opportunity to offer any feedback they may have regarding this session. Facilitators could also encourage students to reflect on the learning that has taken place, using the following conversation prompts:

- Does bullying count as abuse?
- Can you name two specific types of bullying, e.g. homophobic bullying?
- Can you offer the group an example of cyberbullying?

Target setting

The students could be asked to share one piece of information which they have learnt during this session with one individual outside of the group. This could be another staff member or another student.

Compliments to close

This section aims to provide each of the students with a positive affirmation. It will be important for the facilitator to ensure that each student is given a compliment, either by themselves or by another student member of the group.

Relaxation

Mindfulness can be thought of as the ability to remain aware of how you are feeling at that moment. Thinking about the past, blaming or judging yourself, or worrying about the future can often lead to a degree of stress that is overwhelming. But by staying calm and focused in the present moment, you can bring yourself 'back into balance'.

'Mindfulness meditations' can help to bring you into the present by focusing your attention on a single repetitive action, such as your breathing, a few repeated words, or flickering light from a candle.

The students can be asked to engage in the following mindfulness-based activity, with the facilitator reading the following script:

> Please sit quietly and imagine you are on the top of a hill. Look down and see the train track. Picture a train moving past. As you see each carriage go past, think of it as one of your thoughts. If you get caught up in your thought and feel as if you've jumped on to the carriage, gently get back up to the top of the hill. Let that thought 'go' – notice it but don't get on the carriage.

Additional activities

'Read all about it!'

The students can be provided with this article (www.bbc.co.uk/news/health-20582967) regarding the levels of bullying experienced by children with cancer. This activity will also further build upon and develop the students thinking around issues of stereotyping raised in Chapter 4.

- What do they think of this?
- How would they feel if they were in this child's shoes?
- How would they feel if this was their child or sibling?

Spread the news!

Students could be asked to design a poster which illustrates an anti-bullying message. Perhaps this could feature a case study of a bully or a victim.

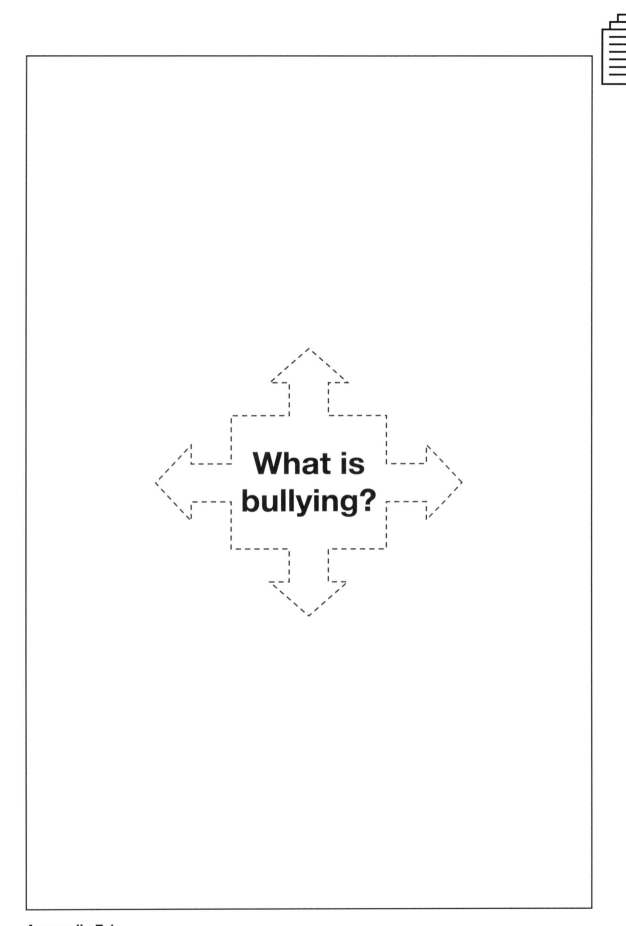

Appendix 7.1

My story board

Chapter 8
Mental health

- Flip chart for group rules
- Picture cards printed, cut out and laminated
- Laptops with internet access
- CD and CD player, or laptop with adjustable volume
- Desired activity sheets

The objective of this session is to introduce the concept of mental health and what constitutes and ensures our well being. One aim of the session is for the facilitators to assess the level of prior knowledge that the students have with regard to mental health. Another is to assist the students in formulating their own ideas about this topic and possibly challenging a few existing ideas. When introducing this topic to the students it will be important to emphasise the definition of physical or mental health as equating to the absence of physical or mental disease.

It may be useful for the facilitators to make reference to some existing definitions in order to both prompt and ensure accuracy of initial thinking around this topic. The World Health Organization (1948) described health as 'a complete sense of physical, mental and social well-being, and not merely the absence of disease or infirmity'. It is something that we should all aspire to and mental health promotion needs to be undertaken for everyone in the community. An initial thought storm activity can encourage the students to formulate their own definitions whilst also allowing for differences of opinion/viewpoints to be aired. It may be useful to prompt students (if necessary) with a list of mentally healthy characteristics as follows:

A sense of well being and contentment.

A zest for living – the ability to enjoy life, laugh and have fun.

Resilience – being able to deal with life's stresses and bounce back from problems/adversity.

Self-realisation – participating in life to the fullest extent possible, through positive relationships and meaningful activities.

Flexibility – the ability to change, grow and experience a range of feelings as the circumstances of one's life change.

A sense of balance in one's life between sociability and solitude, work and play, sleep and wakefulness, and rest and exercise.

A sense of well-roundedness – with attention given to mind, body and spirit.

Creativity and intellectual development.

The ability to care for oneself and others.

Self-confidence and self-esteem.

Young Hearts & Minds (2001) calculated that in every average secondary school of 1,000 students there were likely to be:

- 50 pupils who are seriously depressed
- 100 who are suffering significant distress
- 10–20 pupils with obsessive compulsive disorder
- 5–10 girls with an eating disorder

These figures are clearly accurate and it may be useful to encourage students to investigate these further by visiting the website and downloading relevant publications. It will be important not to sensationalise the figures but rather to point out that such difficulties and problems fall within 'normal' human experience – that is why it is imperative that we all have access to appropriate resources and sources of support. These may include courses such as this one or specific therapeutic interventions conducted by appropriate professionals. What is essential is to highlight the fact that all human beings will benefit from learning about ways to maintain and further foster their physical and emotional well being and that stigmatising people who do have mental health problems is totally unproductive and senseless.

Group rules

At the beginning of each session the group rules should be revisited. The students should be asked if they wish to make any alterations or additions to these rules. It is important that students are able to refer to these throughout the session, therefore they should be placed somewhere in the room where they will remain visible for the duration.

Talk time

As the students may not have another opportunity during their school week to get together in an 'all-female' environment this time should be used primarily to 'catch up'. It could also be used to review the previous session and to introduce the topic of this current session.

Introduction

The facilitator can begin to introduce the topic by asking the students to produce a group definition of what mental health is. To help them along the practitioners could pose the following questions:

Is there such a thing as positive or good mental health?
Can people experience changes in mental health?
Is it possible to spot people with mental health disorders?

The students can also complete the 'Well being self-checklist' **(Appendix 8.1)** as part of this introductory element of the session. This should also foster some discussion within the group as to what is available in terms of professional advice and options. This is important and needs to be developed and reinforced throughout the programme. Being focused on identifying referral routes and procedures for young people to access such services will be important – particularly for a minority of students who may identify some significant issues for themselves in the self-checklist activity. It is essential that these are handled sensitively and that any student identified in this way is provided, at the outset, with some additional time to talk through issues in a 1:1 context – prior to being supported to access further support if this is deemed to be appropriate.

Icebreaker

The students can spread out all of the picture cards **(Appendix 8.2)** featuring different people and lifestyle choices over the table and then be asked to select any individuals who they believe may have a mental health concern or issue. The cards include images of famous individuals who have experienced mental health disorders, images of individuals who belong to different subcultures and images of 'unknown' people in different settings and professions. This activity is designed to show that it is impossible to judge somebody's mental health purely on the basis of their appearance.

Core activity (a)

The students are next encouraged to research a specific mental health disorder using resources such as the BBC Health website (http://www.bbc.co.uk/health/emotional_health/mental_health/). Once they have chosen a disorder they are asked to consider the questions which feature on the accompanying 'Researching mental health concerns' activity sheet in turn **(Appendix 8.3)**.

Core activity (b)

Spread out all of the statement cards **(Appendix 8.4)** over the table and ask the students to separate them into two piles, those they believe to be 'myths' and those they believe to be 'realities'. The aim here is to get the group to come to a unanimous decision. The discussion should continue until all group members are in agreement. Obviously differences of opinion will occur and it is important that the students are able to give and receive gentle challenges. Some may need additional support from the facilitators.

Once the group are in agreement each decision should be justified. Facilitators should have access to the table of 'answers' **(Appendix 8.5)**.

Reflections and feedback

The students should be given the opportunity to offer any feedback they may have regarding this session. Facilitators could also encourage students to reflect on the learning that has taken place, using the following conversation prompts:

How did the students cope with the task set?
If they did not succeed, then how might they be more successful next time?

What would help them to achieve this week's target?
How could they help themselves and each other?

They could also be asked to name something new they have learnt during this session. This finding can be about the session topic or about another group member.

Target setting

The target for this session is for students to make a note in their thought diaries **(Appendix 8.6)** if they come across something, in the media for example, which they recognise to be related to mental health. It is hoped that students will continue to be aware of the issues surrounding mental health once this session has formally come to an end.

Compliments to close

This section aims to provide each of the students with a positive affirmation. It will be important for the facilitator to ensure that each student is given a compliment either by themselves or by another student member of the group.

The students could engage in the closing compliments with each one taking it in turns around the circle to compliment the person on their left. They should be asked to frame these compliments in terms of prosocial skills and engagement in the learning process. Such compliments can initially be modelled by the facilitators. For example:

Libby really helped me when she made that suggestion . . .
Herjit was kind when she said . . .
Jodie really listened to people in the group . . .
Cara didn't put anyone down . . .
Holly was right to tackle us using stereotypes . . .

Relaxation

The technique for this session is listening to music. The students will generally know which genre of music helps them to relax and which genres of music have the alternative effect. The students should be free to play their own choice of music at a reasonable volume. If possible snacks could also be provided and shared.

Additional activities

Spread the news!

Students could be asked to begin to draft a public awareness campaign based on the mental health concern they chose to research during the first core activity. This could include a print advertisement, a 30- or 60-second radio advertisement and a printed leaflet.

Well being self-checklist

Tick next to the statement you feel most accurately describes YOU!

1. **I would describe myself as:**
a. quite a happy and content person who can cope with life's ups and downs
b. rather a serious person who worries a bit but is relatively contented
c. upset, agitated and irritable for most of the time

2. **I generally feel that:**
a. good things tend to happen to me and I'm hopeful about my future
b. I find myself worrying quite a lot about the future
c. I feel that I have few choices in my life and things are more likely to get worse than better in the future

3. **I would describe myself as:**
a. sociable and confident, with lots of good friends
b. sometimes finding it hard to talk to my friends – especially when things are difficult
c. not having many close friends and sometimes not knowing where to turn

4. **Generally, I would cry:**
a. If something happened that made me feel very sad
b. Relatively easily as I can be a little sensitive sometimes
c. Very easily, and often I will cry without knowing why

5. **Mostly my sleep is:**
a. good and I wake up feeling refreshed and energised
b. quite good but sometimes I find it hard to get to sleep and I wake up early
c. disturbed because I don't sleep well or for long enough or I sleep all the time. I don't want to get out of bed in the mornings and simply want to pull the covers over my head and stay there

6. **When I have a lot going on in my life:**
a. I try and keep a balance and still see my friends or do other things I enjoy
b. My friendships and social activities tend to suffer
c. I hide myself away

HOW DID YOU DO?

Mostly a's – you are able to look after yourself well and know when and how to get help. You can talk about your feelings and make sure that you keep a balance between work and social activities. You just need to keep monitoring yourself and setting realistic targets in order to maintain your well being.

Mostly b's – you sometimes feel overwhelmed and don't take care of your emotional and physical needs. You need to make a well being plan for yourself, identifying strategies to keep well and others who can help you. This needs to include keeping an eye on personal stress and using stress busting techniques.

Mostly c's – you are finding life difficult and feel overwhelmed for the majority of the time. You need to talk about these problems with a Mentor/Counsellor and start to develop some self-help strategies. Visit top tips for positive mental health (www.wellscotland.info/top tips) and begin to make a plan. Go for it!

Appendix 8.1

Who has a mental health concern?

Notes

- David Beckham has spoken openly about suffering from Obsessive Compulsive Disorder. His obsessions include counting objects, symmetry and keeping things in order.
- Catherine Zeta-Jones was diagnosed with bipolar II, which differs from bipolar I in that the person never reaches full-on mania.
- Gwyneth Paltrow was diagnosed with depression after her father's death.
- Michael Phelps holds the record for the most Olympic gold models, and he has attention-deficit hyperactivity disorder (ADHD).

Appendix 8.2 Who has a mental health concern?

Researching mental health concerns

What is your chosen mental health concern?

What are the signs and symptoms of this disorder, if there are any?

Can this concern impact upon an individual's physical health?

What are the myths surrounding this diagnosis?

Appendix 8.3

Mental health problems are rare	**Other people can't tell if you have a mental health problem**
People with mental health problems are often violent	**On average, people who experience mental health problems don't live as long**
People can't work if they have a mental health problem	**We all have mental health, like we all have physical health**
People with mental health problems never recover	**People with mental health problems often experience discrimination**

Appendix 8.4

Statement	Myth or Reality	Explanation
Mental health problems are rare	MYTH	Mental health problems affect one in four people in any one year. So even if you don't have a mental health problem, it's likely your best friend, a family member or work colleague will be affected.
People with mental health problems are often violent	MYTH	People with mental health problems are much more likely to be the victims of violence. This myth makes it harder for people to talk openly about mental health problems. It can also make friends reluctant to stay in touch.
People can't work if they have a mental health problem	MYTH	With one in four people affected by mental health problems, you probably work with someone with a mental health problem.
People with mental health problems never recover	MYTH	Many people can and do recover completely from mental health problems. Alongside professional help, the support of friends, family and getting back to work are all important in helping people recover.
Other people can't tell if you have a mental health problem	REALITY	Mental health problems are as real as a broken arm, although there isn't a sling or plaster cast to show for it. Many of those who are affected deal with it alone as nobody else knows.
On average, people who experience mental health problems don't live as long	REALITY	However, it's not the mental health problem that's responsible. The physical health needs of people with mental health problems are often dismissed, causing higher rates of death from heart attacks, diabetes and cancer, for people with severe mental illness.
We all have mental health, like we all have physical health	REALITY	Just like our physical health, our mental health will vary from time to time and it is important that we take care of both.
People with mental health problems often experience discrimination	REALITY	Nine out of ten people with mental health problems experience stigma and discrimination.

Appendix 8.5

My thoughts

		Weekly target
F		
U		
F		

Appendix 8.6

Chapter 9
Anxiety and depression

- Flip chart for group rules
- Desired activity sheets

The objective of this session is to explore anxiety and depression and their physiological, behavioural, emotional and cognitive manifestations. The term 'explore' is pertinent as individuals often have their own understandings and interpretations of the terms, and indeed use them to refer to different things or processes in different contexts and at different times. It may be useful for the facilitators to make reference to some existing definitions in order to enable initial discussions.

Everybody experiences anxiety sometimes, especially when faced with unfamiliar, dangerous or stressful situations. Anxiety is a normal response to a perceived threat, and includes physical, emotional and mental responses, such as an increase in adrenalin, feelings of worry and confusion, and thoughts about danger and catastrophic outcomes. Normal levels of anxiety can assist people to be more focused and motivated, and to solve problems more efficiently. However, chronic or high levels of anxiety can reduce a person's capacity to respond appropriately or effectively to stressful situations or even normal routine activities. For example, a highly anxious person may experience constant physical feelings of panic and may seek to avoid anything that might trigger their anxiety (such as being alone, going to school, talking in front of a group).

ANXIETY TRIGGERS

Anxiety may be triggered in many different ways. Sources of anxiety may include (but are not be limited to):

- fear of social situations
- fears of negative evaluation and rejection
- fear of performing in public
- fear of a specific object or situation (e.g. storms or lightning/thunder, insects, blood)
- fear of being separated from a parent/carer
- fear about a parent/carer being harmed
- fears of harm to self
- fears about academic performance and exams
- fears about starting school or work
- generalised fears about the future (what will happen, how it might turn out).

How to tell if a young person is anxious

Anxiety may manifest as a number of physical symptoms including:

- shaking/ trembling and heart palpitations
- sweating/ flushing or feeling very hot or cold
- feelings of choking
- feeling faint or dizzy
- rapid breathing, feelings of shortness of breath, or breath holding
- difficulty concentrating
- restlessness
- being easily startled
- severe blushing
- numbness or 'pins and needles' in arms and legs
- recurring headaches, stomach aches, backaches
- fatigue
- sleeping difficulties
- going to the toilet more frequently
- muscle tension.

In addition, children and young people experiencing anxiety may display a number of behavioural symptoms including:

- clinging to parents (young children)
- tantrums (young children)
- refusing to go to school
- withdrawing from friends and family
- avoidance of particular object/situation
- being a perfectionist
- being excessively slow
- shyness
- substance misuse
- seeking reassurance
- negative thoughts or pessimism.

Impacts of anxiety

When a young person is quiet and compliant, anxiety symptoms may be overlooked. As a result, they may not receive the help and support they need, which may lead to increasing problems with anxiety in adolescence and adulthood. As symptoms of anxiety become more entrenched and chronic, an anxiety disorder may develop. Research shows young people with untreated anxiety problems may:

- perform poorly in school
- miss out on important social experiences
- experience depression and relationship problems
- engage in substance abuse.

Anxiety also often co-occurs with other disorders such as depression, eating disorders and attention-deficit hyperactivity disorder (ADHD).

Different types of anxiety disorders

While most of the anxiety that children and young people feel is relatively mild, some children and young people may have chronic anxiety or disorders which may require specialist attention.

When the anxiety experienced by a young person starts to affect their general functioning, they may not just be feeling stressed – they may be suffering from an anxiety disorder.

Anxiety disorders are considered serious mental health problems and are one of the most common types of mental health concerns for children and young people. Anxiety disorders are so common that one in four people will experience one or more anxiety disorders during their lifetime.

What is depression?

Depression is when a child's mood is very low, with no obvious cause.
    Symptoms include:

- depressed mood most of the day, every day
- loss of interest or pleasure in activities
- significant weight loss, when not dieting, or weight gain
- a decrease or increase in appetite
- frequent insomnia or sleeping too much
- extreme restlessness or lethargy
- fatigue or loss of energy
- feelings of worthlessness or inappropriate guilt
- diminished ability to think or concentrate
- recurrent thoughts of death and suicidal thoughts.

Children are likely to seem more irritable than sad, and they are more likely to have insomnia than sleep too much.
    The young person may exhibit the following:

- doesn't want to do the things they usually enjoy
- avoids people
- complain they can't sleep well
- has a change in their eating patterns.

They might start being critical about themselves or say they feel useless. They won't do as well as usual at school, because they can't concentrate and don't have the energy to finish off work.

How is depression diagnosed?

A child psychiatrist or clinical psychologist will talk to the child and the parents to:

- discuss how the child feels and assess the symptoms
- check the symptoms don't have a physical cause, such as a reaction to medication
- check the symptoms aren't connected with a major event such as bereavement.

For a clinical diagnosis:

- the child must have at least five symptoms of depression for at least two weeks.
- at least one of the symptoms must be either depressed mood, irritability or loss of interest.
- the symptoms mustn't be caused by another medical condition or a reaction to medication.

Group rules

At the beginning of each session the group rules should be revisited. The students should be asked if they wish to make any alterations or additions to these rules. It is important that students are able to refer to these throughout the session, therefore they should be placed somewhere in the room where they will remain visible for the duration.

Talk time

As the students don't have another opportunity during their school week to get together in an 'all-female' environment this time should be used primarily to 'catch up'. It could also be used to review the previous session and to introduce the topic of this current session.

If the facilitators wish they could utilise the following conversation prompts:

- How are you feeling now?
- How did you feel at the start of the previous session?
- How did you feel at the end of the previous session?
- Is there anything about this session that you are looking forward to?
- Is there anything about this session that you are not looking forward to?
- Is your week going well?
- If it's not going well, is there anything we can do to change that?

Icebreaker

This activity is titled 'silent statements'. The expected outcome here is that students will be able to share information without the pressure of having to speak.

The facilitator should begin by reading out an example statement such as 'I like Eminem'. Students should raise their hand if this statement is true for them. They should be encouraged to look around the group to see who has raised their hands. The facilitator should make it clear that it is absolutely fine to be the only person in the group with their hand raised and that it is also fine if the statement is true for you, but you do not wish to raise your hand. What is important, however, is that all students engage with the activity by looking around to see who has responded and how.

The activity should begin with 'low risk' statements such as 'I have a dog' or 'I like chocolate' to encourage students to feel comfortable about sharing. Choose a selection from the following statements. They are written from low risk to high risk and back to low risk:

- I don't like coming to school
- Sometimes I feel stressed
- I have lain awake at night worrying about things
- I have seen a website about anorexia
- I have a friend who self-harms
- Someone close to me has died
- Someone close to me has committed suicide
- My parents sometimes argue
- I like myself
- I often have arguments with my friends
- I have a good friend I can talk to
- I feel happy at home.

A co-facilitator may wish to take notes during the activity so that they are able to summarise some facts and figures about the group. For example, five students don't like coming to school, two students have seen a website about anorexia.

Introduction

Formulating a group definition of anxiety and/or depression is a good way of introducing the session topic. Students could jot down any thoughts or ideas they have onto the activity sheets provided **(Appendices 9.1** and **9.2)**. They could then feedback to the rest of the group in order to articulate a defining statement or statements. The agreed group definitions could be displayed on a flip chart. In order to guide their thinking facilitators could pose some of the following questions:

- What are the main sources of anxiety in your lives?
- Are any of these 'everyday' anxieties?
- Which are the most anxiety-provoking, 'big' life events?
- How do you currently deal with small and more significant anxieties in your lives?
- Which coping strategies work best for you?

Core activity (a)

The 'Different types of anxiety disorders' sheet **(Appendix 9.3)** gives details about the different types of anxiety disorders. The idea here is to reinforce the fact that these issues are complex and make the very real distinction between everyday stress (which is normal for us all to experience and manage) and the types of anxiety disorders that demand more specialist intervention and support. Facilitators could lead a discussion surrounding these disorders by posing the following:

- What do you know about these disorders?
- Have you even heard of them before?
- Without naming names, do you know of anyone who has any experience of these disorders (either because they have directly been affected, or because they know somebody who has)?

Core activity (b)

The 'Bust a mood!' information sheet **(Appendix 9.4)** presents students with a series of 'mood busting' strategies which they can use in order to prevent a bad mood from escalating. The students could discuss each strategy in turn, with the facilitators posing the following questions:

- Have you ever done something similar in order to improve your mood?
- Does this sound like something which might work for you?

Reflections and feedback

The students should be given the opportunity to offer any feedback they may have regarding this session. Facilitators could also encourage students to reflect on the learning that has taken place, using the following conversation prompts:

- Have we learnt anything new about anxiety or depression?
- Did this new information surprise us?
- Was there anything we have learnt to be untrue about anxiety or depression?

Target setting

The corresponding target for this week is to continue to consider the positive coping strategies explored in today's session. Students could aim to practise some elements of the coping strategies presented during Core activity (b).

Compliments to close

This section aims to provide each of the students with a positive affirmation. It will be important for the facilitator to ensure that each student is given a compliment either by themselves or by another student member of the group. To facilitate engagement with this the facilitators could offer prompts such as:

- Name one person who you felt contributed really well and tell us what they did.

Relaxation

Relieving everyday anxieties can sometimes be as simple as finding a healthy distraction. Many individuals read novels and other types of fiction to help them 'turn off'. During this session perhaps facilitators could bring in a selection of books. Care should be taken to ensure that the books are suitable for readers of a similar age to the students.

Additional activities

Spread the word!

The students should be presented with the 'Suggestions for parents/carers/teachers' information sheet **(Appendix 9.5)**. The desired audience are adults who are learning to manage anxiety in their children and aiming to teach them that this is an essential life skill. The information sheet provides some ways in which parents/carers can assist children and young people to handle anxiety. The students can read through this information and discuss if these ideas would be relevant or helpful to them. They may also wish to use this information to draft posters aimed at adults who are concerned about their children's anxiety levels.

'Read all about it!'

Students could read through the newspaper article entitled 'Call for happiness lessons as teenage depression increases' (www.theguardian.com/society/2008/sep/10/mental health.happiness). They can then discuss their thoughts on this and answer a series of questions posed by the facilitator. These could include:

- What do you think of this article?
- Do you think this kind of input can help young people manage anxiety and prevent depression?
- Would this work in all schools?

Appendix 9.1

Appendix 9.2

Different types of anxiety disorders

While most of the anxiety that children and young people feel is relatively mild, some children and young people may have chronic anxiety or disorders which may require specialist attention.

When the anxiety experienced by a young person starts to affect their general functioning, they may not just be feeling stressed - they may be suffering from an **anxiety disorder.**

Anxiety disorders are considered serious mental health problems and are one of the most common types of mental health concerns for children and young people. Anxiety disorders are so common that one-in-four people will experience one or more anxiety disorders during their lifetime. The anxiety disorders include:

- **Generalised Anxiety Disorder (GAD)** – Excessive and persistent anxiety about events and activities related to work, study, health, finances, family issues or other general concerns. People who have GAD have difficulty controlling worry, and the associated physical and emotional symptoms such as restlessness, fatigue, difficulties in concentrating, muscle tension and sleep disturbance. GAD affects approximately 5% of people at some point in their lives.

- **Panic Attacks and Panic Disorder** – Panic attacks include multiple physical and cognitive anxiety symptoms in the absence of an external threat. A panic attack can include shortness of breath, accelerated heart rate, trembling, sweating, dizziness, and fear of going crazy or dying. Fear of panic attacks in public places may lead to agoraphobia. Panic disorder is recurrent and unexpected panic attacks and persistent fears of repeated attacks.

- **Obsessive Compulsive Disorder (OCD)** – OCD is recurrent and persistent thoughts, impulses or images that are intrusive and unwanted (obsessions), and repetitive and ritualistic behaviours or mental acts that are time consuming and distressing (compulsions) e.g. fears of contamination or harm to self or others; excessive hand washing, showering, checking, or repeating routine actions. OCD affects about 3% of people at some point in their lives.

- **Post Traumatic Stress Disorder (PTSD)** – PTSD may develop after exposure to a distressing and traumatic event or ongoing traumatic situation. Recurrent thoughts, images and nightmares of the trauma occur, as well as changes in mood. Other symptoms include emotional reactivity, memory and concentration difficulties. Around 8% of people are affected by PTSD at some point in their lives.

- **Social Phobia** – anticipatory worry and avoidance of social and performance situations, due to fears of scrutiny and judgement by others, and fear of behaving in a way that is embarrassing or humiliating. Physical anxiety symptoms commonly occur.

- **Specific Phobia(s)** – this is when a person feels excessively fearful of a particular thing or type of situation. Phobias can start at any age and a person may have more than one phobia. Common phobias include:

  o claustrophobia or fear of small spaces such as fitting rooms

  o zoophobia or fear of animals

  o acrophobia or fear of heights such as flying.

Appendix 9.3

Bust a mood!

When you feel a bad mood starting, there are six things you can do to stop it taking over.

1. Catch the thought

Thought catching. What can you say to yourself to stop that bad mood from getting worse?

2. Act fast

What one thing can you do now to begin to sort out the situation so that it doesn't get worse?

3. Distract yourself

Do something else. What can you do now to get your mind off the situation that has prompted your bad mood?

4. Do something different

Take your mind off it. Talk about something else with a friend. How can you make that happen? What can you discuss that will help change your mood?

5. Complete an act of kindness

Do something for someone else. When people do things for other people they have more meaning in their lives and feel better than when they do things for themselves. What could you do?

6. Exercise

Get moving. Take some exercise so that you can't think about that bad mood. What will you do?

Work with a partner to identify four more strategies you can use.

Appendix 9.4

Suggestions for parents/carers/teachers

Learning to manage anxiety is an important life skill. The following are some ways in which parents/carers can assist children and young people to handle anxiety:

- **Support them to challenge underlying beliefs and thoughts** – negative and irrational beliefs and thoughts such as, 'if I don't look perfect, no one will like me', or 'I can't cope with difficult or scary situations', are significant factors in generating anxiety. Model and communicate effective ways to question and challenge anxiety-provoking thoughts and beliefs.

- **Support them to accept uncertainty** – uncertainty is one thing that people worry about a lot because of the potential for negative outcomes. As it is impossible to completely eliminate uncertainty, you can assist children and young people to be more accepting of uncertainty and ambiguity.

- **Be a role model** – if you can manage your own anxiety, young people will see that it can be managed and incorporate your strategies into their own behaviours. Teaching parents to manage their own anxiety has been shown to be helpful in reducing their children's anxiety.

- **Be patient** – sometimes the behaviours of anxious children and teens may seem unreasonable to others. It is important to remember that an anxious young person who cries or avoids situations is, in fact, responding instinctively to a perceived threat. Changing avoidant behaviours takes time and persistence.

- **Balance reassurance with new ideas** – when a child comes to you with something they are worried about, listen and understand what is happening. Explore with them what they could do to manage their fears.

- **Show children and young people some simple relaxation techniques** – deep breathing, progressive muscle relaxation and meditation can be helpful as a way of learning how to better manage physical anxiety symptoms. Generally these techniques are only effective if practised consistently over several weeks.

- **Encourage plenty of physical exercise and appropriate sleep** – when people are well-rested and relaxed, they will be in a better mental state to handle fears or worries.

- **Moderate the consumption of caffeine and high sugar products** – caffeine products including cola and energy drinks increase levels of anxiety as they cause energy levels to spike and then crash. This leaves a person feeling drained and less able to deal with negative thoughts.

- **Make time for things that the child enjoys and finds relaxing** – these could be simple things like playing or listening to music, reading books or going for walks.

- **Help them to face the things or situations they fear** – learning to face their fears and reduce avoidance of feared objects and situations, is one of the most challenging parts of overcoming anxiety. Facing fears usually works best if it is undertaken gradually, a step at a time.

- **Encourage help-seeking when needed** – make sure that children and young people know there are people who can help if they find that they can't handle a problem on their own. Knowing that they can call on others for support if needed will make them feel less anxious about what might happen in the future.

- **Ask for a referral from your GP** – you may have to do this if you suspect a child is suffering from an anxiety disorder. By assisting children and young people to learn effective ways to handle anxiety, you can ensure that they are able to deal with it later in life.

Appendix 9.5

Chapter 10
Stress

Resources required

- Flip chart for group rules
- Post-it notes and pens for the icebreaker activity
- Laptop with internet access, games materials or magazines and books, depending on the chosen option for 'free time'
- Desired activity sheets

The objective of this session is to explore stress and its physiological, behavioural, emotional and cognitive responses. The term 'explore' is pertinent as individuals often have their own understandings and interpretations of the term, and indeed use it to refer to different things or processes in different contexts and at different times. It may be useful for the facilitators to make reference to some existing definitions in order to enable initial discussions into what stress is.

Definitions of stress fall into three categories or models (Bartlett, 1998). One defines stress in terms of an external stressor giving rise to a stress reaction within an individual. Another defines stress in terms of what happens within that individual, in terms of their physiology as a result of this stress reaction. And the third represents a blend between the two. It acknowledges stress as arising from an interaction between the individual and their environment, but also recognises the importance of perception and how this relates to individual differences in what causes stress reactions, how and how much stress is experienced, and how people attempt to cope.

A second objective is to provide students with an opportunity to experience various methods of coping with stress. It is important here to clarify what is meant by coping strategies and how these differ from methods of stress management. Stress management refers to a range of formal psychological techniques used in quite a purposeful way and often in a professional setting, whereas coping strategies, such as turning to others for help and emotional support, are employed frequently and informally by individuals in an attempt to reduce the level of stress they are experiencing.

Group rules

At the beginning of each session the group rules should be revisited. The students should be asked if they wish to make any alterations or additions to these rules. It is important that students are able to refer to these throughout the session, therefore they should be placed somewhere in the room where they will remain visible for the duration.

Talk time

As the students may not have another opportunity during their school week to get together in an 'all-female' environment this time should be used primarily to 'catch up'. It could also be used to review the previous session and to introduce the topic of this current session.

If the facilitators wish they could offer the following conversation prompts:

How are you feeling now?
How did you feel at the start of the previous session?
How did you feel at the end of the previous session?
Is there anything about this session that you are looking forward to?
Is there anything about this session that you are not looking forward to?
Is your week going well?
If it's not going well, is there anything we can do to change that?
Is there anything you are looking forward to this week?

Introduction

Formulating a group definition of stress is a good method of introducing the topic. Students could jot down any thoughts or ideas they have onto the 'What is stress?' activity sheet **(Appendix 10.1)**, and then confer with the rest of the group in order to articulate a defining statement or statements. The agreed group definition could be displayed on a flip chart. In order to guide their thinking facilitators could pose some of the following questions:

What are the main sources of stress in your lives?
Are any of these 'everyday stressors'?
Which are the most stressful, 'big' life events?
How do you currently deal with small and more significant stressors in your lives?
Which coping strategies work best for you?

Icebreaker

The objective of this activity is to illustrate that stress is not always unhealthy. Some stressors such as the pressure felt by athletes shortly before they compete, can affect behaviour in positive ways. For example, it might make them train harder. Experiencing stress shows that you care. For example, feeling stressed because your bus is late when you have an appointment to get to shows that you are concerned about keeping people waiting, which is a positive quality.

For this short activity one facilitator should write feelings and behaviours associated with stress onto Post-it notes. Example statements could be:

'I feel stressed and it's affecting my health'
'I feel stressed but I'm not sure why'
'I can't stop biting my nails because I'm stressed'
'I feel stressed and it's preventing me from sleeping'
'I feel stressed but others think I'm being silly'.

Each facilitator should place one Post-it note somewhere on their person so that it is visible to the rest of the group. Each statement should be discussed by the group. For example, a discussion based around the last statement ('I feel stressed but others think I'm being silly') could focus on the importance of moderators such as personality, outlook and gender, and the impact they have on how and why we experience stress. Two individuals facing the same stimulus, such as having to introduce themselves at a new school, might react differently. The first may be shy and therefore feel stressed at the thought of having to introduce themselves, whereas the other might be more confident in this sort of social situation. Again it is important to highlight that the stress experienced here shows that the individual is concerned about making a good impression, which is certainly a positive quality.

Core activity (a)

Initially it may be useful for the facilitators to determine which coping strategies the students are aware of. A coping strategy can be defined as a plan of action or a behaviour which is followed, either in anticipation of encountering a stressor or as a direct response as it occurs, which is effective in reducing the level of stress experienced. Perhaps students could be asked to complete the 'Coping strategies' activity sheet **(Appendix 10.2)** by offering three more examples (six examples are already given). If possible time could also be spent considering unhealthy coping strategies such as smoking or overeating. Students could be asked to complete the 'Unhealthy coping strategies' activity sheet **(Appendix 10.3)** by, again, offering an additional three examples.

Core activity (b)

Once the facilitators have gained insight into which strategies the students are familiar with, alternative healthy coping strategies can be introduced and experienced. Which strategies are explored obviously depends on available resources. If possible a tutor could be brought in to demonstrate hand massage techniques. The activity could begin with a discussion focusing on the benefits of hand massage and massage techniques in general. A simple demonstration of the basic movements associated with hand massage could then be given by the tutor, allowing learners to then carry out the practical basic movements of the hand massage on one another. An element of peer assessment could also be introduced with the students having to offer feedback. In addition, facilitators could also complete an observation checklist **(Appendix 10.4)** for each student, which could then be placed in their files. Other coping strategies which could be introduced and experienced are reading, drawing, doodling, yoga and running.

Reflections and feedback

The students should be given the opportunity to offer any feedback they may have regarding this session. Facilitators could also encourage students to reflect on the learning that has taken place, using the following conversation prompts:

How did you feel at the start of this session?
Do you feel any different now?

Do you feel you have learnt something about stress today?

Is there anything we did today that you would like more of?

Is there anything we did today that you would like less of?

Target setting

The corresponding target for this week is to continue to consider the positive coping strategies explored today. Students could practise some elements of the coping strategy presented during the core activity. For example, during hand massage it is important to maintain a quiet and calm atmosphere.

Compliments to close

This section aims to provide each of the students with a positive affirmation. It will be important for the facilitator to ensure that each student is given a compliment either by themselves or by another student member of the group. To facilitate engagement with this, facilitators could offer prompts such as:

Name one aspect of this session which you enjoyed.

Name one aspect of this session which you have found useful.

Whose company have you really enjoyed this week?

Whose company do you feel you have benefited from?

Relaxation

No relaxation technique is identified for this session because of the nature of the core activity. Perhaps students could instead be offered 'free time'. Options could be internet browsing, playing quick games (see Additional activities) or reading.

Additional activities

Rules and instructions for the 'Who am I?' game

- Pick one name for each person playing. Don't let any of the players see the names until the game starts.
- The names should represent real people the students are likely to know (celebrities, animated characters, storybook characters, etc.). Some examples could be: Cheryl Cole, Harry Styles, Rihanna, Kate Middleton, Harry Potter, Maggie Simpson and Zac Efron.
- Stick one Post-it note on each player's forehead. Do not allow them to see the name before you put it there.
- Each person gets 20 'yes or no' questions to find out who they are. For example initial questions are often 'Am I female?' or 'Am I male?'
- The players have to roam around the room to ask other players the questions. They can't ask only one player all the questions; the point is to mingle. Whoever guesses correctly using 20 or fewer questions first wins the game.

Rules and instructions for the cereal box game

- Cut or tear the top and bottom flaps off of a cereal box so you are left with a tall, hollow cereal box.
- Place the box in the centre of the room far away from any pieces of furniture. (Move things out of the way if you have to.)
- In order, each player will need to approach the box, bend forward and pick it up with their teeth. Only their feet may touch the floor, and only their mouth may touch the box. Players can bend their bodies any way they like in order to pick up the box. No part of their body (other than the feet) may touch the floor. Falling over or touching the floor ends in disqualification.
- That was easy, right? Now it gets complicated. Next, cut an inch wide strip off the height of the box to make it shorter and have everybody take another turn.
- Continue cutting and playing until there's only one player left.

'Stress slips'

For this additional activity the students are presented with a number of 'stress slips' **(Appendix 10.5)**. These should be cut out prior to the session so that they can be spread out over the table during the session. The students are then asked to read through each statement and rank them from the most stressful to the least. They can then compare their findings with one another, as each student is likely to have the statements arranged in a different order. This activity aims to illustrate that stress is person-specific, in that what stresses one person might not stress another. There is also a 'table sheet' **(Appendix 10.6)** available if the students wish to glue their stress slips down in their ranked order. These completed table sheets can then be placed in the students' individual files.

The 'Four basic stress busters'

This activity sheet **(Appendix 10.7)** is intended both as an activity sheet and as a reference tool, meaning the students should be able to keep these activity sheets in their folders so they can refer back to them when needed. Facilitators should introduce the four basic stress busters as follows:

1 Problem solve
  Decide what is causing the stress and make a plan to tackle it
2 Nurture yourself
  Have a special treat, spoil yourself or indulge yourself
3 Show your feelings
  Talk to a friend, let off steam, sing or write a poem
4 Actively get distracted
  Do something sporty, find an exciting hobby or engage your brain.

Using the activity sheet, students will then be able to identify times when they might use each of these strategies, clarifying exactly what they might do in each of these situations. Here facilitators should be mindful of the differences between healthy and unhealthy responses to stress. Nurturing yourself with a nice hot bath is a healthy response whereas nurturing yourself with a bottle of gin is not.

What is stress?

Appendix 10.1 What is stress?

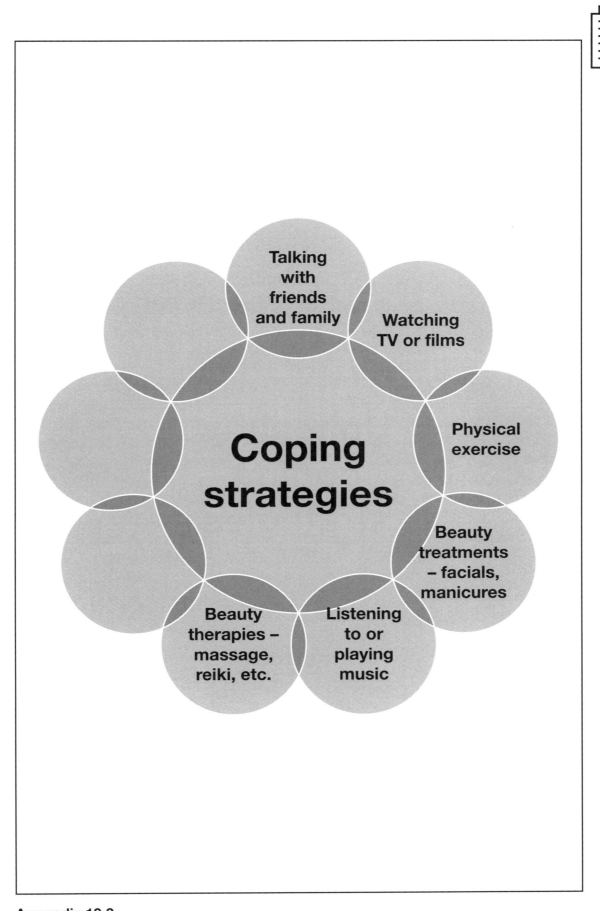

Coping strategies

Talking with friends and family

Watching TV or films

Physical exercise

Beauty treatments – facials, manicures

Listening to or playing music

Beauty therapies – massage, reiki, etc.

Appendix 10.2

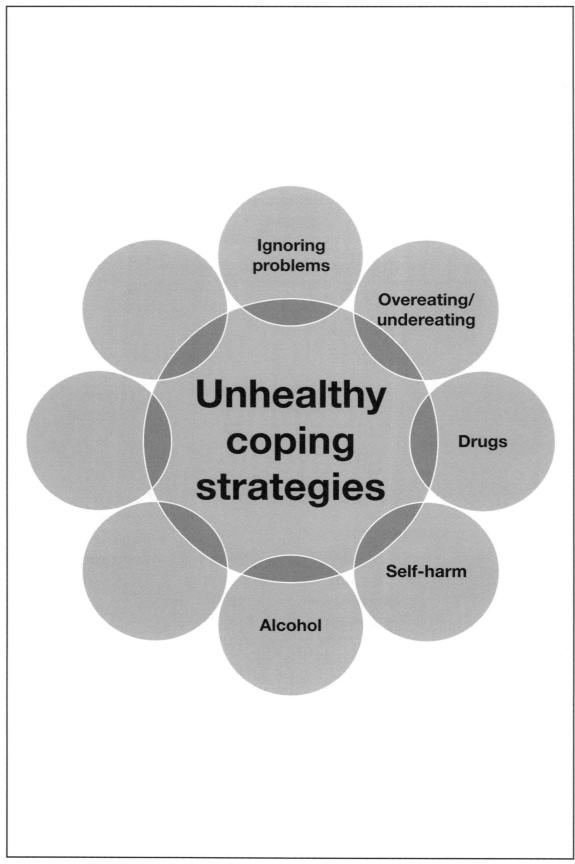

Appendix 10.3

Observation checklist for Hand Massage

Candidate Name.. Date......................

Candidates are not permitted to use the checklist to work from when completing the practical tasks, but may familiarise themselves with it prior to a treatment.

		Tick when observed
1	Selected appropriate work area	
2	Ensured work area is clean, safe and fit for purpose	
3	Selected appropriate products and materials with supervision	
4	Prepared self and/or client	
5	Carried out a visual inspection of hand and nails with supervision	
6	Remove any existing nail varnish (if appropriate)	
7	Carried out a hand massage	
8	Ensured client comfort at all times (if appropriate)	
9	Followed safe and hygienic working practice	
10	Communicated in a professional manner	
11	Behaved in a professional manner	

Assessor's comments if required:

Candidate has successfully completed	Yes/No
Name and Signature of assessor:	Date:

Appendix 10.4

School work

Being bullied

Parents/carers arguing

My appearance

My relationship

Friends falling out with me

Parents/carers splitting up

My sexuality

Peer pressure

My future

Appendix 10.5

1	Most stressful
2	
3	
4	
5	
6	
7	
8	
9	
10	Least stressful

Appendix 10.6

KEEP CALM

AND

PROBLEM SOLVE

When could I do this?

What could I do?

When could you use these strategies? Identify a stressful situation and state how you would deal with it by using each strategy.

KEEP CALM

AND

SHOW YOUR

FEELINGS

When could I do this?

What could I do?

Appendix 10.7a

KEEP CALM

AND

NURTURE

YOURSELF

When could I do this?

What could I do?

When could you use these strategies? Identify a stressful situation and state how you would deal with it by using each strategy.

KEEP CALM

AND

GET DISTRACTED

When could I do this?

What could I do?

Appendix 10.7b

Chapter 11
Self-harm part 1

- Flip chart for group rules
- Paper fish (enough for one per student), two plates, two magazines and a copy of the game instructions (printed and laminated if required)
- Desired activity sheets
- 'Self-harm' cards printed and laminated and 'continuum' cards printed and laminated
- Plain white paper (A1 or A2), a variety of coloured pens and pencils, laptops with internet connection, and a copy of the Good poster checklist for each student in the group

This session looks at actions and activities that may be engaged in by young people and begins the debate as to what constitutes deliberate self-harm and which behaviours, if any, show suicidal intent and which if any, can also be described as 'socially acceptable'. At the outset facilitators should remain mindful. Self-harm is undoubtedly the most challenging area faced by professionals working with young people today. Although it's almost impossible to say how many young people are self-harming, data often suggests that around 10 per cent of young people may try and hurt themselves on purpose at some point, but the figure could be much higher.

Group rules

At the beginning of each session the group rules should be revisited. The students should be asked if they wish to make any alterations or additions to these rules. It is important that students are able to refer to these throughout the session, therefore they should be placed somewhere in the room where they will remain visible for the duration.

It may be pertinent to forewarn some students about the content of this session. The facilitators may wish draw particular attention to the agreed safe places where the students can withdraw to at any time.

Icebreaker

Due to the nature of this session it may be beneficial if the talk time and icebreaker activities swap places in the session plan. The aim of this activity ('Flying fish!') is to create a comfortable, unthreatening and exciting context in which students can begin to relax in order to subsequently engage in the session activities. Prior to the session a 'paper fish' should be cut out of coloured paper for each student, using the template provided **(Appendix 11.1)**. A set of instructions for this game can be found in **Appendix 11.2**. The items and equipment needed to play are also listed.

Talk time

As the students may not have another opportunity during their school week to get together in an 'all-female' environment this time should be used primarily to 'catch up'. It could also be used to review the previous session and to introduce the topic of this current session.

It is important to provide the students with an opportunity to talk 'around' the topic of self-harm for some time before they are required to address a specific point or key issue. The facilitators could ask the students to work in pairs or small groups in order to consider the following questions:

Does everybody self-harm in some way?
When does self-harming become an issue to worry about?
Does the media/internet encourage some forms of self-harming? If so, in what way?

These groups could then feedback their initial thoughts, whilst the facilitators make notes regarding key ideas or recurrent themes on a flip chart.

Introduction

It may be useful at this point for the students to complete the 'The ways in which we self-harm' thought storm activity sheet **(Appendix 11.3)**. This short activity encourages the students to consider what constitutes deliberate self-harm and which behaviours, if any, they had previously overlooked as methods of self-harm. A few examples have already been provided. If the students are struggling to name other methods of self-harm then the following behaviours could be provided by the facilitators as further examples:

Abusive relationships, deliberate starving, dangerous sports, drinking, taking laxatives, smoking cannabis, sunbed use/sunbathing, steroids, overeating, playing on the railway, over-exercising, cutting, smoking, speeding, hair pulling, burning, hitting/ punching, unprotected sex, picking scabs, nail biting.

Core activity (a)

For this activity it may be an idea to clear a space on the table. The facilitators could then place the self-harm cards in the centre of the table. These can be found in **Appendix 11.4**. The self-harm behaviours include:

Deliberate starvation, excessive drinking, drug taking, sunbed use or sunbathing, over-exercising, overeating, cutting, smoking, speeding, dangerous sports, drinking, taking laxatives, playing on the railway.

The facilitators should go through each card, discussing each behaviour briefly with the group in order to ensure a shared understanding. Then the 'Suicidal intent' card

(Appendix 11.5) should be placed at one end of the table, with the 'No suicidal intent' card being placed at the other. Again the facilitators should discuss these terms briefly with the group to ensure a shared understanding.

The students should then be asked to decide where to place each self-harm card on the line between 'Suicidal intent' and 'No suicidal intent'. Facilitators may have to lead discussions. Some statements may trigger more in-depth debates than others. For example, everybody knows that smoking can kill you, therefore is a person who smokes self-harming? If so, does this form of self-harm show strong suicidal intent or reckless-ness? A similar activity involving the 'Socially acceptable' and 'Socially unacceptable' cards **(Appendix 11.6)** could also take place. It is important for the facilitators to emphasise that there are no 'correct' answers. This activity is based on the value judgements of individuals and of the group as a whole, all of which need to be valued and respected.

Core activity (b)

The students could be asked to draft a self-harm awareness poster. For this they will require plain white paper (size A1 or A2) and a variety of coloured pens and pencils. Laptops could be provided so that students are able to research material using the following websites:

http://www.mind.org.uk/
www.thesite.org/mental-health
http://www.nhs.uk/conditions/Self-injury

It may also be helpful to present the students with the 'Good poster checklist . . .' **(Appendix 11.7)** so that they can evaluate the effectiveness of their poster as they go. It may also be beneficial for these posters to be displayed around the room but the facilitators should consider whether or not this in appropriate in their individual contexts.

Reflections and feedback

The students should be given the opportunity to offer any feedback they may have regarding this session. Facilitators could also encourage students to reflect on the learning that has taken place, using the following conversation prompts:

Have your thoughts about what constitutes self-harm altered in any way during this session?
Why do we think people engage in self-harm?
Can all forms of self-harm discussed in this session be addictive?
Why do you think some people resort to self-harming?

Target setting

The students could be asked to think back over all the previous sessions and consider which of the relaxation techniques they have enjoyed, which have been the most effective and which they would like to revisit. They could record their thoughts in their thought diaries. During the following session facilitators could ask students to feedback any thoughts. If a number of students wish to revisit the same techniques then this should be noted by the facilitators.

Compliments to close

This section aims to provide each of the students with a positive affirmation. It will be important for the facilitator to ensure that each student is given a compliment either by themselves or by another student member of the group. During this session the compliments could focus on the engagement of others during the session. The facilitators could use the following conversation prompts:

Who do you feel has really engaged with this session?
Who has made a positive contribution to the session?

Relaxation

The technique for this session is visualisation. Facilitators could introduce the method using the following steps:

- Before you begin it is important to relax. Get comfortable by loosening clothes, taking off footwear and restrictive jewellery. Lying down on the floor, take a few minutes to relax, breathing in and out in slow, deep breaths.
- When you are ready to start, imagine yourself in a calming place such as sitting on a white sandy beach.
- The place you choose could be special to you, your grandparent's garden, for example. It should be a place where you feel you are safe to let go of anxiety and tension.
- The key is to fully engulf yourself in the calming place by using all of your senses. You should be able to hear, see, smell and feel the beach. This will help to induce the calming effect.

Additional activities

Myths vs. realities

The aim of this activity is to explore the perceptions within the group regarding self-harm. Facilitators could begin by spreading the five statement cards **(Appendix 11.8)** out over the table, reading each one aloud in turn. The facilitator should ensure that before moving on to the next card the statement is fully explained to the students. All five statements represent commonly held myths about self-harm and the people who self-harm, although the students should not be informed of this at this stage. The students could then be asked to separate the cards into two groups according to which cards represent myths and which cards represent truths. Once a group consensus has been reached the facilitator could then initiate a discussion into the reasoning behind each classification. The following article includes explanations of each myth which could be used by the facilitators to clarify any misconceptions held by the students (http://selfharm.co.uk/get/myths).

N.B. If this activity is to run during the session, facilitators should ensure that these cards are printed and laminated prior to the start of the session.

I'm a winner!

This activity involves pairs of students engaging in discussions about times when they felt really positive or proud of themselves. Once the students have been paired up they could be provided with the activity sheet **(Appendix 11.9)**.

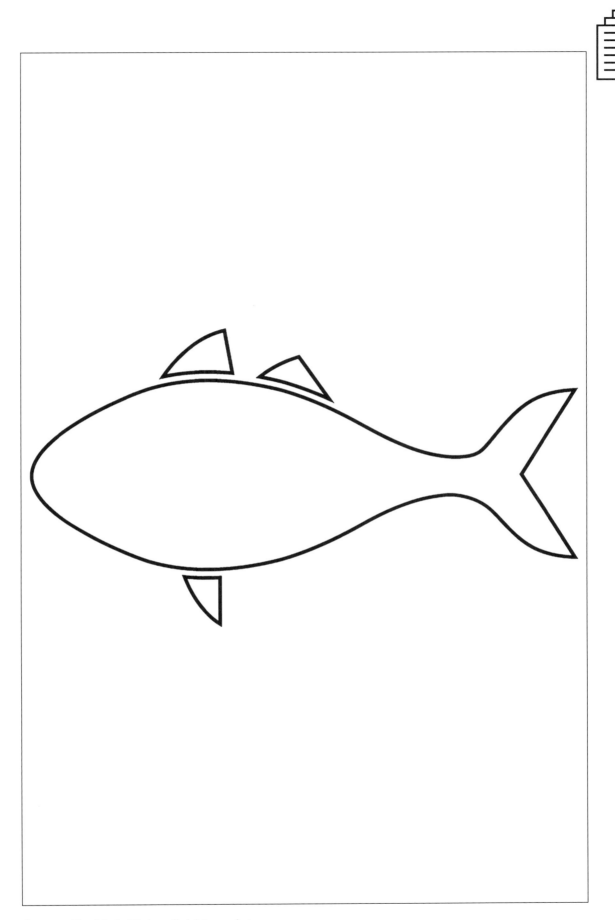

Appendix 11.1 Flying fish! template

Flying fish?

Each player will need a fish.
Each team will need a magazine and a plate.

1. Separate group into two teams, or more if the group is particularly large.
2. Teams line up at one end of the room behind player one.
3. Place two plates on the floor for the 'finish line'.
4. On the word 'Go' player one from each team places their fish on the ground and begins fanning it across the room using the magazine until it reaches the plate.
5. This player then runs back to their team and passes on the magazine to the next player (player two) who puts their fish on the ground and starts fanning it towards the plate.
6. The game continues in this way until all players in the team have successfully fanned their fish all the way from the start to the finish line.
7. The winning team is the first team to finish.

Appendix 11.2

Appendix 11.3

Deliberate starvation

Excessive drinking

Drug taking

Sunbed use or sunbathing

Over-exercising

Overeating

Smoking

Cutting

Speeding

Taking part in dangerous sports

Drinking

Taking laxatives

Playing on the railway

Appendix 11.4

Suicidal intent

No suicidal intent

Appendix 11.5

Socially acceptable

Socially unacceptable

Appendix 11.6

Good poster checklist...

✓ *Does my poster have a title?*

✓ *What is the theme of my poster?*

✓ *Are my sentences properly punctuated and all my words spelled correctly?*

✓ *Do I have a good balance between words and images?*

✓ *Is my arrangement simple yet eye-catching?*

✓ *Finally, what could I do differently next time? Listen to feedback from other students.*

**People who self-harm must
enjoy it or they wouldn't do it**

**People who self-harm
are mentally ill**

**People who self-harm
want to die**

**People who self-harm
are attention seeking**

**Self-harm is just
a girl thing**

Appendix 11.8

I'm a winner

In your pairs decide who is going to talk first and who is going to listen.

Speaker: Think back to a time when you have felt positive or proud of yourself. Describe what happened to your partner.

Listener: Listen carefully to your partner. Encourage them by asked questions when appropriate, e.g. which qualities or talents helped you to achieve your special moment?

Now swap roles and repeat the activity!

Appendix 11.9

Chapter 12
Self-harm part 2

Resources required

- A copy of the 'Would you rather . . .' questions
- Activity sheets as required

Group rules

At the beginning of each session the group rules should be revisited. The students should be asked if they wish to make any alterations or additions to these rules. It is important that students are able to refer to these throughout the session, therefore they should be placed somewhere in the room where they will remain visible for the duration.

It may be prudent to note down any additional rules that might be needed when talking about cutting behaviours such as use of language, sharing personal information, and sharing information which others have told you in confidence.

Talk time

As the students may not have another opportunity during their school week to get together in an 'all-female' environment this time should be used primarily to 'catch up'. It could also be used to review the previous session and to introduce the topic of this current session.

Icebreaker

This activity is titled 'Would you rather . . .' Facilitators should begin by indicating an imaginary line across the floor. Students should be asked to stand along this line, facing forward with one foot either side. Depending on their preferences, students should jump either to the left or right of this line. As the 'Would you rather . . .' questions below are read out, the facilitator should indicate which side of the line represents which response, for example left for broccoli, right for cauliflower. The questions are as follows:

Would you rather:

1 Eat broccoli or cauliflower?
2 Watch daytime TV or Saturday night TV?
3 Have a holiday at the coast or in a city?
4 Be invisible or be able to read minds?
5 Be hairy all over or completely bald?

6 Go without Sunday lunch or takeaways for one year?
7 Be too hot or too cold?
8 Be three inches taller or three inches shorter?
9 Be stranded on a desert island alone or with someone you don't like?
10 See the future or change the past?

This activity is intended to 'relax' the students into the session as they begin to learn new yet neutral things about others in the group. It is also hoped that engaging in light physical activity at this stage of the session will help the students engage with the planned activities.

Introduction

During the last session behaviours such as burning, scratching, banging or hitting body parts, interfering with wound healing, hair-pulling and the ingestion of toxic substances were explored as examples of self-harm. The most common form of self-harm is skin-cutting.

Core activity

This activity aims to explore the ways in which cutting can benefit self-harmers. It is important that the students acknowledge that cutting can help those who choose to self-harm but also that it is an unhealthy coping strategy. The relief that comes from cutting doesn't last very long as it doesn't help address the issues that make self-harmers want to cut in the first place. It also brings with it its own issues and dangers.

The first activity sheet, 'The ways in which cutting can help . . .' **(Appendix 12.1)**, lists six ways in which cutting can help those who self-harm. These include:

- Expressing feelings you can't put into words
- Releasing the pain and tension you feel inside
- Helping you feel in control
- Distracting you from overwhelming emotions or difficult life circumstances
- Relieving guilt and punishing yourself
- Making you feel alive, or simply feel *something*, instead of feeling numb.

The students are then asked to read an excerpt from *Between the Lines* by Victoria Pendleton, the Olympic cycling champion. They are then asked to consider the reasons behind why this person began to cut, using the statements listed above as a reference tool.

The next activity sheet **(Appendix 12.2)** reveals to the students where the quotes are taken from and who is responsible for them. Some discussion points are suggested including:

Does this surprise you?
If so, why?
What does this tell us about those who cut?

The final activity sheet, 'If cutting helps, then why stop?' **(Appendix 12.3)**, lists a number of discussion points which could be used to help facilitate a discussion into the negative aspects of cutting. There are also a small number of 'speech bubbles' for students to record any key thoughts or ideas that arise from the discussion.

Reflections and feedback

The students should be given the opportunity to offer any feedback they may have regarding this session. Facilitators could also encourage students to reflect on the learning that has taken place, using the following conversation prompts:

What have we learnt about self-harm?
Have our views changed after participating in these last two sessions?
How would we now help a friend who was self-harming and where would we advise them to seek support? Where would we not advise them to go for information or help?
How comfortable do we now feel when talking about self-harm?
Do we think that raising these issues with young people will help to reduce the stigma?

Compliments to close

This section aims to provide each of the students with a positive affirmation. It will be important for the facilitator to ensure that each student is given a compliment either by themselves or by another student member of the group.

Relaxation

The relaxation for this session can take the form of a mindfulness activity in which the students are asked to visualise a train track at the bottom of a hill beneath them. They are required to then look at the trains running over the tracks and to place all their thoughts one by one into the train carriages. They should not think about the content of these thoughts or make any value judgements about them but should simply 'let them go'.

Additional activities

X-treme problems!

This activity sheet **(Appendix 12.4)** features a problem scenario in which a young girl is experiencing issues relating to self-harm. The students could be asked to consider what advice they might give to the 'writer'. They could also consider ways in which the writer might address this issue. If the students need further assistance, perhaps the facilitators could offer the following suggestions:

- Begin by acknowledging how distressing or difficult the situation is.
- State how positive it is that she is talking to someone because of the feelings of embarrassment and shame often associated with cutting.

- Advise on how she can help her friend by being aware of what to do if she has harmed in a way that is potentially dangerous.
- Reassure her that people who self-harm normally do not wish to kill themselves.
- Remind her how important it is that she doesn't forget herself in all of this. Perhaps direct her to groups that can support her.

The second problem scenario is included if required.

Getting help, four ways

This additional activity involves the students drafting a poster and/or an information leaflet designed to encourage those who cut to seek help. The 'four ways' of getting help refer to the following points. These could be used by the students to inform the content of their posters.

Tell someone
Admitting to or talking about cutting is often the hardest step. But once you open up to somebody you trust you may feel a great sense of relief. If it's too difficult to bring up the topic in person, write a note.

Identify the issues that are triggering the behaviour
As illustrated during the core activity, cutting can be a way of releasing the pain and tension you feel inside. Try to figure out what feelings or situations are causing you pain and tension. Identify the issues you are having and then tell someone about them. Many people have trouble figuring this part out on their own. This is where a professional can be helpful. A list of useful contacts can be found on the Mind website (www.mind.org.uk).

Ask for help
Tell someone that you want help dealing with your issues and the cutting. If the person you ask doesn't help you get the assistance you need, ask someone else. Self-harm can be a tricky subject for people to talk about. Sometimes adults might try to dismiss or downplay the problems you are facing. If you get the feeling this is happening to you, find another adult!

Work on it
Most people who are in distress need to work with a counsellor or mental health professional to sort through strong feelings, and to learn better ways to cope. One way to find a therapist or counsellor is to ask your GP.

The ways in which cutting can help . . .

It is important to acknowledge that for those who self-harm, cutting helps them, otherwise they wouldn't do it. Some of the ways in which cutting can help include:

- Expressing feelings you can't put into words
- Releasing the pain and tension you feel inside
- Helping you feel in control
- Distracting you from overwhelming emotions or difficult life circumstances
- Relieving guilt and punishing yourself
- Making you feel alive, or simply feel something, instead of feeling numb.

Below are a few quotes taken from a book written by somebody who used to self-harm. Do you recognise any of the points above in the excerpt? Why do you think this person used to self-harm?

'The first time, I used the knife almost thoughtlessly. I did not sit down and decide, consciously, to cut myself. It was almost as if, instead, I slipped into a trance. I held the Swiss Army knife in my right hand, feeling the solid weight, as if it promised something beyond the empty ache inside me.'

'A shiny blade traced a faint line on the pale skin of my left arm. It didn't hurt, as I had yet to add any pressure. The slight indentation was at least three inches above my wrist. I had no wish to cause myself lasting damage; and there was no thought of me using the knife to open up the blue veins in my wrists.'

'I did not want to kill myself. I just wanted to feel something different. Pressing down harder, I had a sudden urge to make myself bleed.'

Appendix 12.1

These quotes were taken from *Between the Lines* by Victoria Pendleton. Victoria is a world and Olympic cycling champion who specialised in the sprint, team sprint and keirin disciplines.

Discussion Points

Does this surprise you?

If so, why?

What does this tell us about those who cut?

For further information, see Pendleton, V. (2012) *Between the Lines.* London: HarperSport.

Appendix 12.2 A self-harming celebrity

If cutting helps, then why stop?

Consider the following questions:

Those who cut experience only temporary relief – what comes next?

Does this 'temporary relief' come at a cost?

Does cutting help address the issues that made the self-harmer want to cut themselves in the first place?

Are there any physical risks? Is it possible that a self-harmer could hurt themselves badly, even though they didn't mean to do it?

Can cutting be addictive?

Main discussion points

Appendix 12.3

X-treme problems!

Dear Agony Aunt,

My friend has started self-harming but she won't talk to anyone about it. She's told me and a few of our other friends. We all want to help but she just won't open up to anyone else and I don't see what we can do. I'm worried she could commit suicide. Please help me.

x

Appendix 12.4a

X-treme problems!

Dear Agony Aunt,

I'm pretty sure my younger sister is cutting herself but she won't admit it. I've seen marks on her arms but when I ask her about them she says there's nothing wrong. Please help, I'm worried that she'll be mad if I say anything but what if I get into trouble for not telling anyone?

X

Appendix 12.4b

Chapter 13
Using therapeutic tools from CBT

Resources required

- Flip chart for group rules
- Activity sheets as required

This session aims to explore the ways in which cognitive behavioural therapy (CBT) can be of use in supporting the emotional well being of the students involved in the programme for girls. Although some activities (especially those included as part of the self-esteem session) are underpinned by principles of CBT, the activities included in this session are specific strategies and skills taken directly from this therapeutic approach.

CBT is currently the 'therapy of choice' (Holmes, 2002: 1). The delivery of CBT has become a central part of recent government initiatives (Department of Health, 2011a, b), due to findings from random controlled trials indicating it is potentially seen as being more cost effective than medication (DfES, 2003). This report, alongside *Every Child Matters*' emphasis on children's health and well being (DfES, 2003), has led educational psychologists in particular to question their position in the provision of psychotherapy for children's mental health issues (Woods & Farrell, 2006; Mackay, 2002) and whether CBT can be incorporated into educational psychology casework (Dunsmuir & Iyadurai, 2006; Greig, 2007; MacKay & Greig, 2007). Many therapists, counsellors, mentors and SENCOs are currently making use of CBT approaches in order to support positive change and emotional well being in the students they support. This kind of approach is a specific goal-orientated therapy, and it frequently results in positive change within a relatively short period of time. This is very unlike traditional psychotherapy, which can, for some individuals, take many years to produce any kind of positive result or outcome.

CBT reveals the role that thoughts play in relation to both our emotions and our behaviours. This approach provides individuals with a way of talking about themselves, their world and people who inhabit it, so that they are more able to understand how what they do affects both their thoughts and feelings, and vice versa.

This advocates that change in thought processes can have a significant effect upon altering behaviours. Unlike many of the talking treatments that traditional therapists have used, CBT focuses upon the 'here and now', as well as ways to improve the individual state of mind in the present time. This is innovative in the sense that there is no focus on the causes of distress or past symptoms as there evidently is with traditional psychotherapy.

RESTRUCTURING THOUGHT PROCESSES

Young people are frequently flooded with anxious and negative thoughts and doubts. These messages will often reinforce a state of inadequacy and/or low levels of self-esteem. The process of CBT helps to support young people in reconsidering these negative assumptions. It also allows them to learn how to change their self-perceptions in order to improve their mental and emotional state – this is the key aim of this kind of intervention. Changing negative thought patterns or opinions will ultimately help young people to become more able to control and change their behaviours, but this does take practice. This is why, as with anger-management interventions, another key element of the approach is the requirement to learn, and to put into practice, the skills or strategies discussed in any session.

ABC

The CBT approach breaks the problems into smaller parts. This enables the student to see how they're connected and how they affect them. This follows a process of A, B, C, as follows:

- A, or the activating event, is often referred to as the 'trigger' – the thing that causes you to engage in the negative thinking.
- B represents these negative beliefs, which can include thoughts, rules and demands, and the meanings the individual attaches to both external and internal events.
- C is the consequences, or emotions, and the behaviours and physical sensations accompanying these different emotions. It is important to highlight and discuss with the students how the way that they think about a problem can affect how they feel physically and emotionally. It can also alter what they do about it. This is why the key aim for CBT is to break the negative, vicious cycle that some students may find themselves in. For example, if you think that you will get your work wrong you feel angry, and then you don't give it a try in case it is wrong.

CORE BELIEFS

Core beliefs are the strong, enduring ideas that we may have about ourselves. This kind of belief system gives rise to rules, demands or assumptions which in turn produce automatic thoughts. Core beliefs generally fall into three main categories: beliefs about yourself; beliefs about other people in the world; beliefs that are either positive or negative. What is important is to identify our core beliefs and to also consider why these may or may not be unhelpful. In this way we can begin to identify negative automatic thoughts (NATs).

WHAT ARE NATS?

Negative core beliefs can cause us to engage in a number of faulty thinking strategies. Individuals will tend to focus on NATs. Some of these thoughts that students may hold about themselves could include the following:

- I always look ugly.
- I don't understand this work.
- He thinks I'm stupid and an idiot.
- She gave me a nasty look.
- I'm just such a useless person.
- I can't do that and I'll never be able to do it like other people can.

When working with students in identifying such faulty thinking, the main aim is to encourage them to break the negative cycle. These NATs can arise from a number of errors in our thinking, including the following six types of faulty thinking:

- Doing ourselves down – only focusing on the negatives and seeing bad things about ourselves.
- Blowing things up or catastrophising – making things worse than they really are.
- Predicting failure – setting your mind ready to predict failure at all costs.
- Overemotional thoughts – this is when your emotions become extremely powerful and cloud your judgement.
- Setting yourself up – setting yourself targets that are too high so that you know then you will fail.
- Blaming yourself – thinking that everything that goes wrong is your own fault.

When working with young people, it is important to allow them time to consider the effects that these NATs can have, prior to them beginning to implement some changes.

BEHAVIOURAL EXPERIMENTS

One of the most helpful interventions for developing new and more positive belief systems, and for challenging these negative automatic thoughts, is to test the evidence. Students can engage in the following questioning process:

- What is the evidence for this thought?
- What is the evidence against this thought?
- What would my best friend say if they heard my thought?
- What would my teacher say if he heard my thought?
- What would my parents or carers say if they heard my thought?
- What would I say to my best friend if s/he had this same thought?
- Am I making mistakes? For example, blowing it up, forgetting my strengths or good points, self-blaming or predicting failure or thinking that I can mind read what others are thinking?

This kind of strategy is particularly useful in terms of reinforcing the need to gather accurate evidence. What we believe about ourselves is not always true. It is not how others always see us and these kinds of beliefs need to be challenged in this way. Using this sort of questioning process, and gathering evidence in the form of such a behavioural experiment, is a particularly positive strategy for beginning to identify and challenge unhelpful beliefs that students may carry.

Group rules

At the beginning of each session the group rules should be revisited. The students should be asked if they wish to make any alterations or additions to these rules. It is important that students are able to refer to these throughout the session, therefore they should be placed somewhere in the room where they will remain visible for the duration.

Talk time

As the students may not have another opportunity during their school week to get together in an 'all-female' environment this time should be used primarily to 'catch up'. It could also be used to review the previous session and to introduce the topic of this current session.

Icebreaker

This activity is titled 'My beliefs: a guessing game'. Each group member is given a piece of paper and then writes down three things that they believe in. These are folded and collected by the facilitators and put into a container and jumbled up. Each member of the group then takes out a piece of paper and reads out the three beliefs. Other students in the group then try to guess who wrote it and state why they arrived at their decision. The relevant individuals will then admit ownership of these beliefs and then expand on what these beliefs mean to them. This activity aims to encourage listening skills and also tolerance, acceptance and respect for difference.

Introduction

The facilitators could ask the students to work in pairs or small groups in order to consider the following questions:

- Does everybody need to change in some way?
- When does negative thinking become an issue to worry about?
- Does the media/internet encourage some forms of negative thinking and putting ourselves down? If so, in what way?

These groups could then feedback their initial thoughts, whilst the facilitators make notes regarding key ideas and recurrent themes on a flip chart.

Core activity (a)

The first two activity sheets **(Appendices 13.1** and **13.2)** are intended to act as an introduction to CBT, providing the students with some visual prompts as to what the processes are based upon. The link between how we think and how these thoughts then affect our feelings and behaviours is made explicit. The idea here is for students to be able to make these links and realise that CBT is all about using skills to prevent the development and continuation of negative patterns of thinking and behaviour.

Core activity (b)

This activity, 'A good time and a bad time' **(Appendix 13.3)**, encourages students to further reflect upon both a good and a bad time in their lives and to further analyse the connections and links between their thinking, feeling and behaviours.

Reflections and feedback

The students should be given the opportunity to offer any feedback they may have regarding this session. Facilitators could also encourage students to reflect on the learning that has taken place, using the following conversation prompts:

- How are what we think, what we do and how we act related?
- If what we think is negative how do we challenge it?
- Why is it important to look at the evidence which supports these thoughts?

Target setting

Students could be asked to make a note in their thought diaries **(Appendix 13.4)** of any time they resort to 'faulty thinking'.

Compliments to close

This section aims to provide each of the students with a positive affirmation. It will be important for the facilitator to ensure that each student is given a compliment either by themselves or by another student member of the group.

Additional activities

Core beliefs

This 'Core beliefs quiz' activity **(Appendix 13.5)** encourages the students to identify what they really think about themselves and the consequences of their behaviours and actions. The idea here is to then identify any of these beliefs which might not be so helpful. For example, if I think that being bad will gain me attention then this may not be so helpful – particularly in the school context.

Faulty thinking

The students are next presented with the 'Faulty thinking information sheet' and questions **(Appendix 13.6)**. The information sheet describes some of the ways we may engage in faulty thinking. The students can discuss these in turn and perhaps begin to identify times when they may have engaged in these types of faulty thinking. The question sheet asks them to answer a series of questions and these are intended to be a type of behavioural experiment in which students attempt to identify the evidence for and against their particular thoughts. The idea here is to reinforce the importance of gathering accurate information and feedback – particularly when we may be adopting negative and erroneous views of ourselves and our behaviour.

Cognitive behavioural therapy (CBT)

A set of tools to help you deal with problems and find the best solutions.

Looking at links...

What you think

What you do

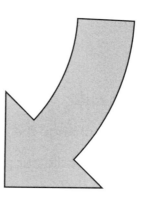

How you feel

Appendix 13.1

How do the LINKS work?

Some examples:

Think... ⇨	Feel... ⇨	Think... ⇨
I'm useless at meeting new people	I feel scared and nervous when I meet new people	I'm useless at meeting new people
No one in my form likes me	I feel sad and angry	I avoid going out at break and start to bunk off school
I'm rubbish at Maths	I feel dumb and fed up	I stop trying because I know I'll get it all wrong

Statement: How you think about something will become true
Stop, Think and Reflect!

o   Is this true?

o   Can we change the way we think?

o   Can we handle our problems differently to change how we feel and what we do?

o   Can we gain more CONTROL over what happens to us in our lives?

Appendix 13.2

Think about your most recent... good time!
Complete the circle, whether by drawing pictures or by writing text.

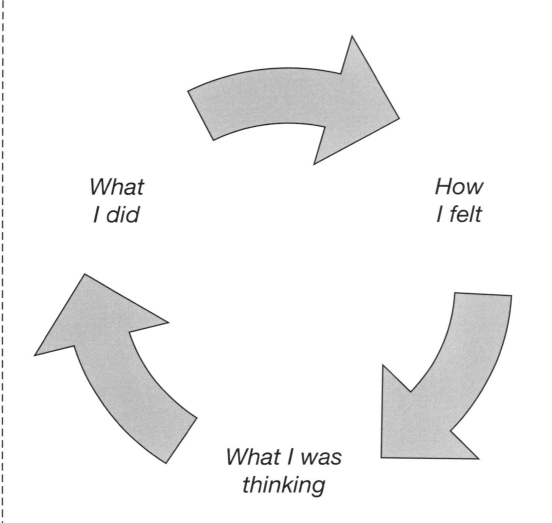

What I did

How I felt

What I was thinking

Can you do the same for a recent bad time?

Appendix 13.3

My thoughts

	Weekly target
F	
U	
F	

Appendix 13.4

Core beliefs quiz

Have a go at this quiz! What do you think will happen in each situation? Stop, think and reflect and then TALK it through.

IF .... THEN ....

If I am bad then
_____

If I get it wrong then
_____

If I work hard then
_____

If I am kind then
_____

If I have friends then
_____

If I am good then
_____

If I make people feel good then
_____

If I don't have friends then
_____

If I let people down then
_____

If I think positively then
_____

Which beliefs are HELPFUL? Why?

Which beliefs are UNHELPFUL? Why?

Appendix 13.5

Faulty thinking information sheet

There are six kinds of faulty thinking

(1) DOING DOWN!	(2) BLOWING UP!
<ul><li>Only focus on negatives.</li><li>Only see the bad bit in something that was good overall.</li><li>Not counting a positive, e.g. 'he only wants to go out with me because he can't find anyone else'.</li></ul>	<ul><li>Making things worse than they are.</li><li>It's all or nothing, e.g. I only got 78% and not 100% – it's not good enough!</li><li>Magnifying the problem, e.g. I got the answer wrong and everyone in the class laughed at me! It's a catastrophe! I'll never get over it!</li></ul>
(3) PREDICTING FAILURE!	**(4) OVEREMOTIONAL THOUGHTS**
<ul><li>Mind reading to predict failure, e.g. I bet they are all laughing at me! I know he hates me!</li><li>Fortune-telling – knowing you will fail, e.g. I know I won't be able to do that work/I know they won't like me.</li></ul>	<ul><li>With this faulty thinking our emotions become very strong and cloud the way we think and understand things.</li><li>Because we feel bad we presume everything is – the emotions takeover!</li><li>We attach negative labels to ourselves, e.g. I'm rubbish, stupid, a loser.</li></ul>
(5) SETTING YOURSELF UP!	**(6) BLAME YOURSELF**
<ul><li>Setting targets too high and setting ourselves up to fail.</li><li>I should, I must, I can't, I want, I shouldn't, etc.</li><li>Creating an impossible standard to achieve.</li></ul>	<ul><li>Everything that goes wrong/is wrong is our fault – even, stuff we have no control over! E.g. I got into my car and it broke down! I turned on the computer and it crashed!</li></ul>

Appendix 13.6a

Key Questions

- What is the evidence 'for' this thought?

- What is the evidence 'against' this thought?

- What would my best friend say if they heard my thought?

- What would my teacher say if he/she heard my thought?

- What would my parent/carer say if they heard my thought?

- What would I say to my best friend if he/she had this thought?

- Am I making any thinking mistakes? (e.g. blowing it up, forgetting my strengths or good points, self-blaming or predicting failure/thinking I know what others are thinking, etc.)

Key Points

GET IT IN PERSPECTIVE!!

We need the evidence – check it out!

Be realistic – life is not problem-free!

Challenge and change your thinking to cope more effectively.

Appendix 13.6b

Chapter 14
Parenting

Resources required

- Flip chart for group rules
- Desired activity sheets

This chapter introduces the concept of parenting and seeks to investigate the qualities and skills needed to take on this role. The students are presented with a wide range of activities which should generate debate and thinking around all of the key issues. What is important is to encourage their views and ideas to be articulated rather than imposing those which may not resonate with their own experiences.

According to the Church of England's Children's Society, all children should be taught good parenting in schools (Layard & Dunn, 2009). In the most far-reaching enquiry into childhood in the UK, they found that today's youngsters are under more stress than any previous generation, because of family breakdown, increasing commercial pressures and exam stress, leaving them 'anxious and troubled'.

The report, led by the former Downing Street adviser Richard Layard and Judith Dunn, a developmental psychologist, also found that one in three children live apart from their fathers by the time they reach the age of 16. Even by the age of three, children in single-parent homes are more likely to show signs of poor behaviour. The report does suggest ways to improve the quality of parenthood. These include lessons in personal and social education at school to cover the skills of parenting, relationships and child development.

Before the child is born, the parents should be fully informed of what is involved in bringing up a child, not only the physical demands and sacrifices but the emotional demands and the stresses as well as the joys it will bring to their own relationships.

Layard & Dunn (2009)

Group rules

At the beginning of each session the group rules should be revisited. The students should be asked if they wish to make any alterations or additions to these rules. It is important that students are able to refer to these throughout the session, therefore they should be placed somewhere in the room where they will remain visible for the duration.

Talk time

As the students may not have another opportunity during their school week to get together in an 'all-female' environment this time should be used primarily to 'catch up'.

It could also be used to review the previous session and to introduce the topic of this current session.

It may also then be helpful to reflect on the following questions:

What do you think makes a good parent?
What makes a bad parent?
Is there such a thing as a 'perfect' parent?
Discuss this sentence – 'all parents mess up their children, just in varying degrees'.

Icebreaker

This activity follows a round-table format. If space permits, students could be asked to sit in a large circle in the centre of the room. This provides the facilitator with an opportunity to mix up friendship groups so that students are sitting next to students they might not know quite as well.

The students are given just a few minutes to talk with each other to try and find three things they have in common, e.g. we both like hot chocolate. If students choose to share things about themselves relating to any of the session topics this is fine but by no means essential.

Led by the facilitator, each pair then feeds back to the whole group and each participant should be encouraged to speak. The facilitator may conclude by summarising any key themes and identifying any similarities and differences.

Introduction

By way of an introduction students could be asked to complete the 'Good parenting' thought storming activity sheet in **Appendix 14.1**. Students could consider the importance of good parenting and what good parenting involves. Facilitators should let the students take the lead on this, aiding the resulting discussion as opposed to driving it.

Core activity (a)

This activity is entitled 'Eight signs of bad parenting'. Initially the students could make reference to the series of bad parenting pictures in **Appendix 14.2**, using the information sheets in **Appendices 14.3** and **14.4**. These images are downloaded from the internet and are readily available. Students can discuss why some people (perhaps those who posted them) may find them funny, whilst others may view them as forms of abuse. They can then consider the eight signs in turn and discuss what each one might mean in reality to a child.

Core activity (b)

Refer students to the article on fathers' role and right to paternity leave taken from a national newspaper (http://www.independent.co.uk/voices/commentators/mary-ann-sieghart/mary-ann-sieghart-get-new-fathers-to-stay-at-home-with-the-baby-and-we-all-gain-7743402.html). They can read through this article and then consider the following:

Is it a good thing for fathers to have time at home after the birth of a baby?
Does having a baby affect a father's working life as much as a mother's?
What do you think about stay-at-home fathers?
Why do children need fathers and is it different for boys and girls?

Reflections and feedback

The students should be given the opportunity to offer any feedback they may have regarding this session. Facilitators could also encourage students to reflect on the learning that has taken place and to review the progress they made in relation to last week's target. The following conversation prompts could be used:

How did you cope with the task set?
If you did not succeed, how might you be more successful next time?
What would help you to achieve this week's target?
How could you help each other?

They could also be asked to name something new they have learnt during this session about the role of a parent.

Target setting

The target for this session is for students to make a note in their thought diaries **(Appendix 14.5)** if they come across something, in the media for example, which they recognise to be related to 'bad parenting'. It is hoped that students will continue to be aware of the issues surrounding bad parenting and its impact upon the lives of children once this session has formally come to an end.

Compliments to close

This section aims to provide each of the students with a positive remark. It will be important for the facilitator to ensure that each student is given a compliment either by themselves or by another student member of the group.

The students can then engage in the closing compliments, with each one taking it in turns around the circle to compliment the person on their left. They should be asked to frame these compliments in terms of prosocial skills and engagement in the learning process. Such compliments can initially be modelled by the facilitators.

Relaxation

The facilitator will need to be in a quiet room with no distractions and to provide the students with chairs so that both feet can be planted firmly on the ground and legs uncrossed. They will need to place their hands in their laps, close their eyes and follow the following instructions, which can be read to them (by the facilitator or a designated student) in order:

Clench your fists – hold them, feel the tension, then let your fingers loose and relax. Feel yourself relax all over. Then repeat.

Bend from your elbows and tense up your biceps. Feel the tension, then put your arms out and let them relax. Repeat. Really feel the tension and the relaxation in your muscles.

Straighten up your arms so that you feel the tension in the upper parts – within the muscles on the backs of your arms. Then let your arms hang loose and feel the tension disappear. Repeat.

Close your eyes extremely tightly. Feel the tension in your eyelids and around your eye sockets. Then relax your eyes – still keeping them closed and enjoy the sensation. Repeat.

Frown and pull the muscles in your forehead together. Then relax and feel your forehead becoming smooth and relaxed. Repeat.

Clench your fists tightly. Relax and open your lips a little. Repeat.

Close your lips together tightly. Then relax and focus on the difference between the relaxed position and the tensed position. Feel yourself relax all over your face, in your mouth and in your throat. Repeat.

Lift your head up and let it drop back as far as you can (without any straining). Feel the tension in your neck. Move your head from left to right and right to left, feeling the tension moving into each side of your neck. Next lift your head forwards and press your chin downwards against your chest. Then return you head to an upright position and relax. Repeat.

Lift your shoulders up and hold in the tension then drop and relax. Feel this relaxation spreading to your back and all the parts of your face and neck. Repeat.

Concentrate on relaxing your whole body and breathe slowly in and out. Each time you exhale imagine all the tension leaving your body. Next breath in, inhale deeply and hold your breath. Then breathe out, feeling your chest relax. Breathe in deeply through your nose, counting slowly to five. Then exhale slowly, letting your breath free to the count of five. Repeat.

Next, tighten up your stomach muscles. Hold your stomach in as tightly as you can and then let the muscles relax. Concentrate on the two different sensations of tension and relaxation. Next push your stomach out and hold in this position prior to relaxing the muscles again. Repeat.

Tighten up your thighs and buttocks and then release and relax. Press down on your heels and then relax. Repeat.

Press your feet into the floor and feel your calf muscles tensing. Release and relax. Repeat.

Bend up your ankles towards your body and hold them tightly. Then release and feel them relax. Repeat.

Curl up your toes as tightly as you can. Hold them tightly. Relax and release them. Repeat.

Finally, let yourself relax all over – from your toes, through your feet, ankles, calves, shins, knees, thighs, hips, stomach and lower back. Feel the tension escape. Relax your upper back, chest, shoulder, arms and fingers. Feel your neck, jaws and facial muscles relax. Breathe in deeply and then slowly let your breath out. Count slowly from 1 to 10 and then open your eyes. You are now truly relaxed.

Additional activities

'The cost of a quickie'

This activity aims to explore the financial demands placed upon new parents. Students should be provided with copies of the activity sheet in **Appendix 14.6**. The activity sheet asks the students to work in groups to estimate the costs involved during pregnancy and the first year of parenting. The total figure should fall somewhere between £3,000 and £3,500.

Teen parents – challenges and advantages

To complete this activity sheet **(Appendix 14.7)** students must think of six advantages and six challenges associated with becoming a teenage parent. Perhaps facilitators could offer the following examples.

Challenges
Difficulty in finishing their education or getting a good job
Difficulty in accessing affordable childcare
Finding the balance between bringing up a family and having a social life

Advantages
Teenagers have lots of energy to keep up with toddlers
Young parents are better at dealing with lack of sleep
Grandparents may be young enough to look after the children.

Good parenting

Appendix 14.1

Appendix 14.2a
Bad parenting?

Appendix 14.2b
Bad parenting?

Appendix 14.3

Q. How to be a good parent?

A. By avoiding the Eight signs of bad parenting

1. Avoiding and Neglecting Your Child

Neglecting a child physically or emotionally can affect them in a negative manner. Child neglect is a very common type of child abuse. Child abuse is more than physical abuse. Ignoring the needs of children, putting them in unsupervised or in dangerous situations, making the child feel worthless, etc. can lead to the child feeling very low about themselves and may lead to loneliness. This can affect the mental health or social development of the child and may even leave lifelong psychological scars.

2. Physical and Verbal Abuse

Exposing a child to physical violence or verbal abuse can be very damaging to their psychology. Many parents are seen venting out their frustrations at their children without realising what sort of psychological damage they are inflicting on the child. Such acts can also lead the child to lose confidence and develop an inferiority complex. Punishment is required when a child does something wrong but when they are extensively punished for even small matters it may lead to them being rebellious.

3. Encouraging Bad Behaviour in Children and Not Disciplining

There are many parents who do nothing to discourage the bad behaviour of their child. As the saying goes, you reap what you sow. If you are someone who shouts or uses bad language in front of your child it is only natural that they would follow in your footsteps. Perhaps that may be the reason why children of parents who drink heavily or smoke find nothing wrong with the habits and may start drinking or smoking at a young age.

4. Favouritism or Partiality

Favouritism or Partiality can be very damaging to a child. In many households boys get preferential treatment, making girls feel useless or neglected. Be it education, food or essential requirements, girls are often known to suffer, starting from their own homes. Many parents even have the habit of complaining to others about their own children. Many have the habit of grumbling or complaining about anything or everything in front of others, rather than dealing with the problem. Parents who are overly criticising and comparing their children with other children are also only causing damage to their own children.

Appendix 14.4a

5. Forcing Choices on Children

It is very true that a parent knows what is best for his or her child. But many times the parents are seen forcing their choices on children without considering the interests, intelligence level or capacity of the child. Many parents are very demanding and look at achieving their own unfulfilled dreams and ambitions through their children. But when the child can't rise to the expectations of the parent it can be very demotivating and disappointing to the child. A child requires encouragement and motivation from parents, and demoralising and demotivating them can affect them adversely.

6. Not Being Wise with Money

Many parents are not very wise with money as far as children are concerned. While some cater to every whim and fancy of the child, others are excessively stingy with money which may result in the child developing the habit of stealing to fulfil their needs. At the same time, those children whose every need is fulfilled may fail to realise the real value of money and may indulge in bad habits. So maintaining a balance is very important.

7. Too Much Pampering or Interfering

Like negligence, too much pampering or worrying about children also can spoil the child by making them too demanding. Many parents protect their children and interfere in their activities in such a manner that when they grow up they become overly dependent on others or grow up as cowards.

8. Not Trusting the Child

Many parents believe in others more than believing in their own children. Many times they do not even allow the child to give an explanation. Many parents have no faith in their children and demotivate them with their words or actions. This sort of behaviour can cause a child to be a rebel or do things which they are not supposed to do.

In short, there are several signs and effects of Bad Parenting. Many kids lose self-esteem or develop bad habits or feel inhibited for the rest of their lives. Parenting is a continuous job and the children rely on parents for the same. So make it a point to take time out for children, teach them the correct mannerisms and correct them when they do wrong. When parents neglect the set rules and boundaries for children it is only natural for the kids to become brats or display unacceptable behaviour. So it is your choice if you want to be a good and positive role model for the child or be a bad parent.

Appendix 14.4b

My thoughts

	Weekly target
F	
U	
F	

Appendix 14.5

The cost of a quickie!

The following items are all required before birth and during the first year of parenting. Working in groups, can you estimate an average cost for each category?

Remember you are looking at how much money new parents will spend on each category during their pregnancy and the first year of the baby's life. Good Luck!

Pregnancy clothes	**Pregnancy toiletries**
Nursery furniture/decorations	**Cot**
Bedding	**Pram**
Car seat	**Baby carrier**
Changing mat	**Baby bath**
Baby monitor	**Baby skincare products**
Baby wipes	**Steriliser**
Formula milk bottles	**Baby food**
Highchair	**Clothes (first year total)**
Disposable nappies (first year total)	**Safety gates**
Toys/accessories	**Baby bouncer**

TOTAL _____

Which of these items would you need to buy weekly?

Which of these items are essential and which might you be able to do without?

Which of these items could you buy second hand?

Appendix 14.6

Teen parents
Challenges and advantages

1.	1.
2.	2.
3.	3.
4.	4.
5.	5.
6.	6.

Appendix 14.7

Chapter 15
Healthy living

Resources required

- Flip chart for group rules
- Desired activity sheets

Maintaining a healthy lifestyle which includes exercise and a well-balanced diet is not always easy to do but it is essential for adolescents, who are still growing both physically and psychologically. This session highlights the importance of keeping fit via regular exercise and healthy eating plans. Young people need to be encouraged to think about what they gain from regular exercise and making even a partial improvement to their fitness.

Information from the current BBC website highlights and describes some of the main benefits as follows:

Physical inactivity is an independent risk factor for coronary heart disease – in other words, if you don't exercise you dramatically increase your risk of dying from a heart attack.

Conversely, exercise means a healthier heart because it reduces several cardiovascular risks, including high blood pressure.

Being physically active can bolster good mental health and help you to manage stress, anxiety and even depression.

Regular exercise as you age keeps you strong, mobile and less dependent on others.

Regular exercise can help you achieve and maintain an ideal weight, which can be important in managing many health conditions, or may just make you feel happier about your appearance.

All exercise helps strengthen bones and muscles to some degree, but weight-bearing exercise, such as running, is especially good in promoting bone density and protecting against osteoporosis, which affects men as well as women.

Different exercises help with all sorts of health niggles, such as digestion, poor posture and sleeplessness, and physical activity can be beneficial for a range of medical conditions, from diabetes to lower back pain.

There are lots of positive reasons for getting fitter, including meeting new people, discovering new interests and generally feeling better. However, the statistics themselves should help people to make the right decision regarding their healthy living regime:

While in 2007, the Government-commissioned Foresight report predicted that if no action was taken, 60 per cent of men, 50 per cent of women and 25 per cent of children would be obese by 2050, the actual figures are rising ahead of the forecast rate.

Between 1993 and 2008, there has been a marked increase in the proportion of people who were obese, reaching 24 per cent of men and 25 per cent of women in 2008.

The picture is just as worrying for young people – obesity rates were 17 per cent in 2008 among boys, and 15 per cent in 2008 among girls.

Obesity is responsible for 9,000 premature deaths a year in this country, and is a major contributory factor to heart disease.

Coronary heart disease (CHD) is still the leading cause of death in the UK, accounting for about a fifth of all deaths, according to the Office for National Statistics (2013).

About a third of deaths caused by CHD are among people aged under 75.

TEENAGERS AND DIET

It is vital that teenagers' diets should sustain growth and promote good health. During this time, a number of physiological changes occur that affect nutritional needs, including rapid growth and considerable gains in bone and muscle (especially in boys). This is also a time when teenagers begin to develop real independence from their parents, including making decisions about the food they eat. Teenagers often choose food in response to peer pressure or as an act of defiance against parents. However, notwithstanding this fact, there are many opportunities to encourage healthy dietary habits in teenagers, particularly when relating good food choices to sporting or physical prowess.

NUTRITION

The National Diet and Nutrition Survey of Young People Aged 4 to 18 Years (Gregory *et al*., 2000) provides detailed information on the nutritional intake and physical activity levels of young people in the UK.

The findings reveal average consumption of saturated fat, sugar and salt is too high, while that of starchy carbohydrates and fibre is low. During the 7-day recording period, more than half the young people surveyed hadn't eaten any citrus fruits, green leafy vegetables (such as cabbage or broccoli), eggs or raw tomatoes. The survey also showed that one in ten teenagers have very low intakes of vitamin A, magnesium, zinc and potassium. Intake of iron and calcium was also below ideal levels among many of the teenagers.

Meanwhile the rising levels of obesity suggest many young people are eating too many calories.

IRON DEFICIENCY

Iron deficiency is one of the most common nutritional deficiencies in the UK. In the National Diet and Nutrition Survey, up to 13 per cent of teenage boys and 27 per cent of girls were found to have low iron stores. Rapid growth, coupled with a fast lifestyle and poor dietary choices, can result in iron-deficiency anaemia. Teenage girls need to take particular care because their iron stores are depleted each month following menstruation.

The main dietary source of iron is red meat, but there are lots of non-meat sources, too, including fortified breakfast cereals, dried fruit, bread and green leafy vegetables. The body doesn't absorb iron quite as easily from non-meat sources, but you can enhance absorption by combining them with a food rich in vitamin C (found in citrus fruits, blackcurrants and green leafy vegetables). In contrast, tannins found in tea reduce the absorption of iron, so it's better to have a glass of orange juice with your breakfast cereal than a cup of tea.

CALCIUM DEFICIENCY

The survey also highlighted that 25 per cent of teens had a calcium intake below the recommended level, which has serious implications for their future bone health.

Osteoporosis is a disease that causes bones to become brittle and break very easily. Bones continue to grow and strengthen until the age of 30, and the teenage years are very important to this development. Vitamin D, calcium and phosphorus are vital for this process, with calcium requirements for the teenage years ranging from 800 mg to 1,000 mg per day.

Calcium-rich foods should be consumed every day. The richest source of calcium in most people's diet is milk and dairy products. Encourage your teenagers to eat three portions of dairy food each day – for example, a glass of milk, a 150 g pot of yoghurt and a small matchbox-sized piece of cheese.

FOODS TO CHOOSE

Adolescence is a time of rapid growth, and the primary dietary need is for energy – often reflected in a voracious appetite. Ideally, foods in the diet should be rich in energy and nutrients. Providing calories in the form of sugary or fatty snacks can mean nutrient intake is compromised, so teenagers should be encouraged to choose a variety of foods from the other basic food groups:

Plenty of starchy carbohydrates – bread, rice, pasta, breakfast cereals, chapattis, couscous and potatoes

Plenty of fruit and vegetables – at least five portions every day

Two to three portions of dairy products, such as milk, yoghurt, fromage frais and pasteurised cheeses

Two servings of protein, such as meat, fish, eggs, beans and pulses

Not too many fatty foods

Limit sugar-rich food and drinks.

Other important dietary habits to follow during adolescence include:

Drink six to eight glasses of fluid a day.

Eat regular meals, including breakfast, as it can provide essential nutrients and improve concentration in the mornings. Choose a fortified breakfast cereal with semi-skimmed milk and a glass of fruit juice.

Take regular exercise, which is important for overall fitness and cardiovascular health, as well as bone development.

These habits are highlighted within this session which aims to support the students in identifying their own healthy living plans in line with such advice.

Group rules

At the beginning of each session the group rules should be revisited. The students should be asked if they wish to make any alterations or additions to these rules. It is important that students are able to refer to these throughout the session, therefore they should be placed somewhere in the room where they will remain visible for the duration.

Talk time

As the students may not have another opportunity during their school week to get together in an 'all-female' environment this time should be used primarily to 'catch up'. It could also be used to review the previous session and to introduce the topic of this current session.

It may also then be helpful to reflect on the following questions:

How healthy do we feel right now?
How do you measure 'health'?
Would we describe ourselves as physically active?

Icebreaker

For this activity students should be directed by the facilitator to line up one behind the other. If the group is particularly large the group could be split into two lines. The group or groups should then be instructed to form new lines in order of:

Height, from smallest to tallest
Birthdays, from January through to December
Shoe size, from smallest to largest
Alphabetical first names (A–Z)
Alphabetical mothers' first names.

Students could be timed to see how long it takes them to reorganise themselves and to see if they get any quicker as they complete each task. If the group has been split, the two groups could compete against each other to see which is quicker.

Introduction

For this activity students should be provided with the 'My three healthy living essentials' activity sheet **(Appendix 15.1)**. Students are asked to specify three things they undertake in order to 'feel well'. Examples could be washing your hair every day, getting at least 7 hours sleep, not leaving the house without mascara on or keeping fingernails painted. The facilitator should stress that these 'essentials' may well be different for each individual.

Core activity (a)

For this activity each student will require a copy of the 'Healthy diet quiz' sheet **(Appendix 15.2)**. This activity sheet includes five questions about the seven 'building blocks' which are essential when maintaining a healthy eating plan. These are: carbohydrates, 'healthy' fats, proteins, fibre, vitamins, minerals and water. Students could also be provided with copies of the table in **Appendix 15.3** so that they are able to look up for themselves any answers which they are unsure of. Giving students the opportunity to 'research' the answers as opposed to providing them outright may strengthen understanding and increase feelings of achievement.

Core activity (b)

This activity seeks to explore the various benefits associated with physical activity. The activity sheet in **Appendix 15.4** asks students to consider any social, physical or mental benefits which may result from taking part in even light physical exercise. Facilitators could offer the following examples: improved confidence, making friends, stress release, improved posture and improved concentration. Perhaps they could also use the icebreaker activity as an example of light physical activity. This way the students are able to relate the term 'physical activity' to a recent and/or relevant personal experience. It is hoped that students will begin to recognise how much they already know about healthy eating and exercise during these core activities which will help them gain confidence in their level of understanding.

Reflections and feedback

The students should be given the opportunity to offer any feedback they may have regarding this session. Facilitators could also encourage students to reflect on the learning that has taken place and to review the progress they made in relation to last week's target. The following conversation prompts could be used:

How did you cope with the task set?
If you did not succeed, how might you be more successful next time?
What would help you to achieve this week's target?
How could you help each other?

They could also be asked to name something new they have learnt during this session about the importance of maintaining a healthy lifestyle.

Target setting

Students could be asked to consider ways in which they could increase their levels of physical activity on a day-to-day basis. Simple suggestions could include getting off the bus one stop early, meaning you have to walk that little bit further to reach your destination. Students should note down any ideas in their thought diaries **(Appendix 15.5)** for discussion next session.

Compliments to close

This section aims to provide each of the students with a positive remark. It will be important for the facilitator to ensure that each student is given a compliment either by themselves or by another student member of the group. Such compliments could involve highlighting the following behaviours:

Listening well
Showing empathy or concern for others
Being thoughtful
Working hard in activities during the session
Acknowledging the contributions made by others
Overcoming any initial embarrassment or fear, especially during the icebreaker or additional activities and trying to contribute
Having a go and being positive in the session.

Relaxation

Perhaps this session could conclude with the students making simple fruit smoothies for themselves and the facilitators to enjoy together. The following recipe could be used, although there are many similar recipes widely available on the internet.

Ingredients

1 ripe mango
1 ripe banana
3 heaped tbsp Greek-style yoghurt
300 ml/10½ fl oz milk
Ice cubes (optional)

Preparation method

Blend all of the ingredients in a food processor until smooth and well combined.
To serve, pour into two tall glasses.
Aside from ingredients the following equipment will be required:

Food processer
Chopping board
Small knife
Measuring spoons
Measuring jug.

Additional Activities

Race in place

For this activity the facilitator will require a sheet of quiz questions. Students should be asked to stand up and jog on the spot. On the facilitator's signal they should stop running, listen to the question and respond with the answer. The student to answer first wins a point, and the student who finishes the game with the most points is the winner. However, disqualification can occur if the student is jogging when they shouldn't be, or is standing still when they should be jogging!

Spread the news!

Students could be asked to begin to draft a public awareness campaign based on what they have learnt about the relationship between physical activity, a balanced diet and a healthy lifestyle. This could include a print advertisement, a 30- or 60-second radio advertisement and a printed leaflet.

The students could also be provided with laptops so that they are able to research additional material, perhaps using the Change4Life website (http://www.nhs.uk/Change 4Life).

My three healthy living essentials...

Different people have different things that they must do in order to feel well. For example, some women like to wash their hair every day whereas others can go 2 or 3 days without freshly washed hair. What three things must you do in order to feel well?

1.

2.

3.

In this group there is bound to be a degree of variation. Imagine how much variation there would be if the whole student body took part in this activity!

Appendix 15.1

Healthy diet quiz

1. To maintain fluid levels, the body needs

_____

2. Quick release energy is provided by

_____

3. Vitamin D is important for

_____

4. Wholegrain cereals provide considerable supplies of

_____

5. _____

can lead to heart disease

Appendix 15.2

The seven building blocks to a healthy diet

Food type	How does it help?	Where do we get it?
Carbohydrates	Your body uses carbohydrates to make glucose which is the fuel that gives you energy and helps keep everything going	Fruits Vegetables Breads, cereals, and other grains Milk and milk products Foods containing added sugars (e.g. cakes, cookies, and sugar-sweetened beverages).
'Healthy' fats	Provide slow-release energy. Too much saturated fat from animal products can lead to heart disease	Nuts Dairy products Vegetable oils Fish
Proteins	Proteins are part of every cell, tissue, and organ in our bodies. These proteins are constantly being broken down and replaced	Meats, poultry, and fish Legumes (dry beans and peas) Eggs Nuts and seeds Milk and milk products Grains Some vegetables, and some fruits (provide only small amounts relative to other sources)
Vitamins	A – for vision B – for energy production and stress reduction C – to keep skin healthy D – to help bones and teeth	Fruit Vegetables
Minerals	Calcium – to strengthen bones Iodine – for energy production Iron – prevents fatigue	Fruit Vegetables Fish
Fibre	Can't be digested Fills you up and keeps you 'regular' Aids healthy digestion	Fruit Vegetables Wholegrain cereals
Water	Maintains fluid levels Prevents dehydration	The tap!

Appendix 15.3

Physical activity + a balanced diet = *a healthy lifestyle*

What benefits are there to physical activity? Think about mental benefits, social benefits and physical benefits.

Benefits of physical activity

Appendix 15.4

My thoughts

	Weekly target
F	
U	
F	

Appendix 15.5

Chapter 16
Looking forward/evaluation

Resources required

- Flip chart for group rules
- Sheets of plain paper, Sellotape and marker pens
- Desired activity sheets

The purpose of this session is to enable the students to reflect upon the learning undertaken in this programme and to also consider and formulate their own personal plans for future well being.

Group rules

At the beginning of each session the group rules should be revisited. The students should be asked if they wish to make any alterations or additions to these rules. It is important that students are able to refer to these throughout the session, therefore they should be placed somewhere in the room where they will remain visible for the duration.

Talk time

As the students may not have another opportunity during their school week to get together in an 'all-female' environment this time should be used primarily to 'catch up'. It could also be used to review the previous session and to introduce the topic of this current session.

Icebreaker

Each member of the group is required to collect from the facilitator, a sheet of plain paper, a marker pen and a piece of Sellotape or masking tape. The students are all asked to record compliments and positive comments about each individual group member on these sheets which are stuck onto their backs. Once this has been completed and everyone has contributed to everyone else's compliment sheets, the students can then read through these positive comments. It will be useful to allow some time for students to consider how such an activity makes them feel. Are they positive? Are they embarrassed? Do they feel as if their self-esteem has been reinforced or do they feel slightly uncomfortable? Considering why they should experience such feelings may also be part of this reflection process. It will also be helpful for students to consider whether or not others' views of them are different to their own views of themselves.

Introduction

It may be helpful for the facilitator to summarise the key topics and to ask the students themselves what they think that they have learnt throughout this programme. Highlighting the previous chapter titles as follows may prompt thinking here:

1. Introduction
2. Self-esteem
3. Body image and appearance
4. Stereotypes
5. Relationships part 1
6. Relationships part 2
7. Bullying
8. Mental health
9. Anxiety and depression
10. Stress
11. Self-harm part 1
12. Self-harm part 2
13. Using therapeutic tools from CBT
14. Parenting
15. Healthy living

As the development and maintenance of well being has been central to this programme of support it is important to further consider this concept at this conclusion stage of the programme. So, what is it that actually constitutes mental health and well being? The DfES (2001) adopted the Mental Health Foundation's definition of children's mental health, describing the mentally healthy child as one who can:

- Develop psychologically, emotionally, intellectually and spiritually
- Initiate, develop and sustain mutually satisfying personal relationships
- Use and enjoy solitude
- Become aware of others and empathise with them
- Play and learn
- Develop a sense of right and wrong
- Resolve (face) problems and setbacks and learn from them.

This list is further built upon by Helpguide (www.helpguide.org/mental-emotional-health.htm) to also include:

- A sense of well being and contentment
- A zest for living – the ability to enjoy life, laugh and have fun
- Resilience – being able to deal with life's stresses and bounce back from adversity
- Self-realisation – participating in life to the fullest extent possible, through meaningful activities and positive relationships
- Flexibility – the ability to change, grow and experience a range of feelings as life's circumstances change
- A sense of balance in one's life between solitude and sociability, work, play, sleep and wakefulness and rest and exercise
- A sense of well-roundedness with attention to mind, body and spirit

- Creativity and intellectual development
- The ability to care for oneself and others
- Self-confidence and self-esteem.

It may be helpful to provide this information to the students and to engage in a thought storming activity in order to consider their own development and state in each of the above areas. A 'blank' format has been provided **(Appendix 16.1)** which allows the students to decide which area they wish to consider.

Core activity (a)

As stated above, in this final session students are provided with an opportunity to reflect on things they have learnt during the entire course. In leading the discussion the facilitator may find the following questions helpful:

- What have we learnt about well being?
- What are the problems with maintaining well being for young people?
- What was the most useful session? Why?
- What was the least useful session? Why?
- To what extent do we feel better equipped to help ourselves and others maintain well being?
- To what extent do we feel we will be able to avoid negative behaviours ourselves?
- Have any of our opinions about well being changed during the course?
- If you were running this course, how would you change it to make it better next time?

Core activity (b)

In this activity, the students are asked to complete a 'Personal review' **(Appendix 16.2)** in order to identify the development of their skills in terms of managing and sustaining their well being. The focus here is upon the management of stress, anxiety and the reduction in self-harming behaviours. The facilitator will need to highlight the fact that self-harming behaviours do not just equate to cutting but rather cover a wide range of such behaviours including smoking, recreational drug use, binge drinking and eating, not exercising and engaging in frequent patterns of negative thinking. The idea here is to reinforce the need to develop and then maintain well being 'habits' which can then ensure that young people do not develop more serious conditions or engage in more risky behaviours.

The sentence-completion activity asks the students to identify positive and less positive elements of the programme alongside highlighting areas for future learning. They can also support the development of the resource in the future by providing explicit feedback.

Reflections and feedback

The facilitator could conclude by reviewing the work completed during the programme via a whole-group discussion. They could use the following conversation prompts, if they wish:

- Have your thoughts about what constitutes well being altered in any way during this programme?
- Why do we think people engage in risky and unhealthy behaviours?
- Can all forms of risky and self-harming behaviours discussed in this programme be addictive?
- What are the key skills and strategies you have learnt and practised which will help you to maintain your well being in the future?

Target setting

The students could be asked to think back over all the previous sessions and consider which of the self-management techniques they have enjoyed, which have been the most effective and which they would like to revisit. They could record their thoughts in their thought diaries **(Appendix 16.3)**. During the following session facilitators could ask students to feedback any thoughts. If a number of students wish to revisit the same techniques then this should be noted by the facilitators.

Compliments to close

This section aims to provide each of the students with a positive affirmation. It will be important for the facilitator to ensure that each student is given a compliment either by themselves or by another student member of the group.

During this session the compliments could focus on the engagement of others during the session in identifying their own skills and what they have learnt from the programme. The facilitators could use the following conversation prompts:

- Who do you feel has really engaged with this programme?
- Who has made a positive contribution?
- Who has engaged in some real learning?
- Who has made the most progress throughout the programme?
- Who has identified an accurate picture of their learning and future needs?

Celebration

For the final session instead of concluding the session with a relaxation technique perhaps facilitators could lead the students in a celebration. Students should be praised for their engagement with the programme and the progress they have made throughout.

Additional activities

Dear friend . . .

Using the format in **Appendix 16.4**, students could be asked to write letters addressed to those who may be involved with the programme in the future. They should think about what advice they could give them, or if they might benefit from reassurance regarding the content of the programme.

My future self

Students could be asked to complete the activity sheet titled 'My future self' **(Appendix 16.5)**. This aims to encourage the students to look ahead at where they want to be and to consider the ways in which they could work towards this. Targets are also explored to ensure that those set by the students are both reasonable and achievable.

Certificate of achievement

Perhaps these could be presented to the students who have taken part at the end of the final session. A format has been provided **(Appendix 16.6)**.

Appendix 16.1

Personal review

This feedback will not be shared with the group but will provide useful information for your course facilitator/teacher to help them plan future courses.

Rate the following statements on a scale of 1–10

I understand what is meant by 'well being'

1	2	3	4	5	6	7	8	9	10
	disagree			neither agree or disagree			agree		

I can identify my own negative and self-harming behaviours

1	2	3	4	5	6	7	8	9	10
	disagree			neither agree or disagree			agree		

I can identify stressors in my life

1	2	3	4	5	6	7	8	9	10
	disagree			neither agree or disagree			agree		

I have skills for coping with stress and anxiety in my life

1	2	3	4	5	6	7	8	9	10
	disagree			neither agree or disagree			agree		

I could support a friend who is finding it hard to cope

1	2	3	4	5	6	7	8	9	10
	disagree			neither agree or disagree			agree		

I can identify negative automatic thoughts

1	2	3	4	5	6	7	8	9	10
	disagree			neither agree or disagree			agree		

I can name helpful and unhelpful responses to stress and anxiety

1	2	3	4	5	6	7	8	9	10
	disagree			neither agree or disagree			agree		

Appendix 16.2a

My evaluation of the programme...

Finish the following sentences!

The activity I enjoyed most was

_____

The activity I enjoyed least was

_____

Something I have learned is

_____

I would like to learn more about

_____

The most useful part of the course was

_____

The least useful part of the course was

_____

Something I would change about the course is

_____

Any other comments

_____

_____

_____

_____

Appendix 16.2b

My thoughts

	Weekly target
F	
U	
F	

Appendix 16.3

Dear friend,

From,

Appendix 16.4

My future self

Try to imagine yourself in 10 years' time. Where would you like to be?
How do you want to feel? What do you want to be doing? Where would you want to live
and work?

Sketch your 'Ten Years Forward' portrait and record your ideas around the picture frame.

Now think of three things you could be doing now in order to achieve your future goals.
Work with a partner and share your ideas.

Appendix 16.5a

Think about this!

Are your targets/goals for the future…

Small – a 'small' step, a little hill not a mountain

Measurable – something for which you can measure success

Attainable – you can get there and do it

Realistic – it is not something you can't achieve, it is based on reality

Time bound – you have set a review date and know when you will measure your success.

When developing your goal you need to be able to answer the following six questions:

Who will do this/help me?

What will be achieved?

Where will I do this/get help/do 'best'?

Why am I doing this/making this change?

When will I know I've achieved my goal and what is my review date? Specify this!

How will I know I am really successful/need to evaluate and try again?

Appendix 16.5b

Certificate of Achievement

This certificate is awarded to

_____

In recognition of

_____

Date _____ **Signature** _____

Appendix 16.6

APPENDICES

Appendix 1
Information sheet for students

Supporting the Well Being of Girls

Dear student,

During this term we will complete a 16-session programme called 'Supporting the Well Being of Girls'. We hope this information sheet answers some of the questions you may have about these sessions. Please talk to your form tutor or head of year if you would like any further information.

What is Supporting the Well Being of Girls?

This is a 16-session programme which will help you make positive changes in a short space of time. Each session will teach you new skills and strategies which will help your own personal development, and give you the chance to practise these skills and further develop and maintain your well being. These skills will be useful to you throughout your whole lives at school and out of school!

What will I gain by taking part in these sessions?

This programme will help you take responsibility for your own well being rather than focusing on difficulties or problems you may have encountered in the past. You will have the opportunity to clarify your goals and make changes in order to achieve them. You will also learn ways of supporting your friends.

What will be expected of me?

You will be encouraged to listen and respond in group discussions. You will also be asked to try out strategies in each session but you will not necessarily have to share confidential information with the rest of your group. You will be expected to be respectful of others in your class.

Appendix 2
Information sheet for parents/carers

Supporting the Well Being of Girls

What is Supporting the Well Being of Girls?

This 16-session programme is based on the current well being agenda and adopts a range of strategies to promote skills of self-awareness and self-management. This is an approach which is based on solution-building rather than problem solving. It is a goal-oriented approach which can bring about positive change in young people over a short period of time and ensure the development of self-help strategies and personal awareness.

How will my child benefit?

This programme will help your child to identify the strengths, skills and talents which she already has. Girls will have the opportunity to clarify their goals and expectations and take responsibility for their future and well being. The focus will be on developing skills and a knowledge base by which to make positive changes towards achieving their goals.

How are the sessions structured?

All sessions will take place as a group. In each session the group will be taught new skills or techniques which every student will then have the opportunity to practise and refine over time. Peer support is encouraged both inside and outside the sessions. There will be an opportunity for students to evaluate the work themselves at the end of the programme.

What should I do if I have any further questions about the programme?

Please contact the person named on the accompanying letter if you have any further questions or concerns.

Appendix 3
Letter to parents/carers

Supporting the Well Being of Girls

Dear parents/carers,

There is an increasing amount of research that suggests that young people today may experience a range of issues from low self-esteem and anxiety to other behavioural difficulties. The well being of our students is a priority of our school and therefore during this term we will be delivering a 16-session programme called 'Supporting the Well Being of Girls'.

The programme aims to target young people exhibiting difficulties maintaining well being in order prevent escalation of any problems, and to provide them with a range of skills and strategies which will help and support them throughout their lives. Enclosed is an information sheet which will provide more information about the programme.

We hope you appreciate the importance of this programme for the personal, social and emotional development of your child and will support them as they work through the sessions.

Thank you

If you have any concerns about this programme or require any further information please contact:

Mental health

What is mental illness?

There is no precise definition as to what constitutes mental illness but it is considered to be a condition that may affect the way we feel and think, resulting in an inability to cope with everyday social interactions and routines. Although often considered to be rare, as many as one in four adults may suffer from a form of mental health problem every year and these often begin in childhood. The mental health problems suffered by adolescents in our schools include: depression, anxiety, eating disorders, phobias, personality disorders and obsessive compulsive disorders.

What causes mental illness?

Mental illness is a misleading term as many mental health disorders may have a physical or biological component. For example, those who have a close family member who suffers from depression are more prone to it themselves. Some medications and hormonal changes may also lead to forms of mental illness. Environmental and social factors may include poverty, stress and trauma. Often it is a combination of factors that leads to mental illness.

What are the signs of mental illness in young people?

In adolescents, warning signs may include the following:

- Frequent outbursts of anger
- Changes in eating habits perhaps leading to considerable weight gain or weight loss
- A prolonged negative mood
- Frequently complaining of physical problems, e.g. headache, stomach ache
- Challenges to authority such as theft, truancy and vandalism
- Alcohol or drug abuse
- Sleeplessness.

© 2014, *Supporting the Well Being of Girls*, Tina Rae and Elizabeth Piggott, Routledge

How can I improve my own mental health?

- Avoid substances that are depressants, such as alcohol and tobacco or other drugs.
- Allow yourself plenty of time for a form of relaxation you enjoy. Physical exercise is particularly useful in combating depression.
- Eat a healthy balanced diet.
- Talk to others about how you are feeling. Hiding your feelings will not make the problem go away and things may build up.
- Set yourself goals and prioritise your challenges.

How can I get further help?

If you continue to feel depressed or anxious you may need to seek expert help. To do this you should visit your GP who should be able to help you access the support you need. This might include a referral for counselling, medication such as antidepressants or a referral to a community mental health team specialist such as a psychiatrist. It is advisable to seek help early to reduce negative outcomes as a result of your illness.

Appendix 5
Referral routes to specialist agencies

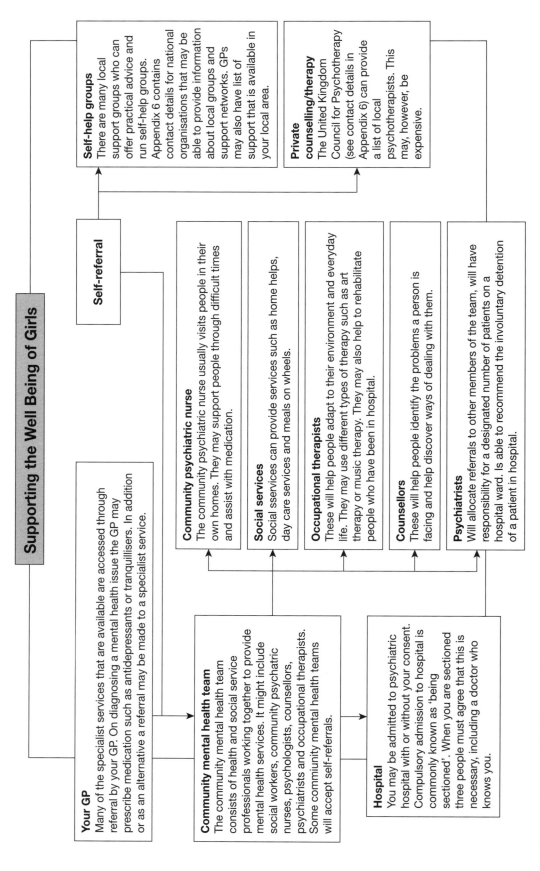

Supporting the Well Being of Girls

Your GP
Many of the specialist services that are available are accessed through referral by your GP. On diagnosing a mental health issue the GP may prescribe medication such as antidepressants or tranquillisers. In addition or as an alternative a referral may be made to a specialist service.

Self-referral

Self-help groups
There are many local support groups who can offer practical advice and run self-help groups. Appendix 6 contains contact details for national organisations that may be able to provide information about local groups and support networks. GPs may also have list of support that is available in your local area.

Private counselling/therapy
The United Kingdom Council for Psychotherapy (see contact details in Appendix 6) can provide a list of local psychotherapists. This may, however, be expensive.

Community mental health team
The community mental health team consists of health and social service professionals working together to provide mental health services. It might include social workers, community psychiatric nurses, psychologists, counsellors, psychiatrists and occupational therapists. Some community mental health teams will accept self-referrals.

Hospital
You may be admitted to psychiatric hospital with or without your consent. Compulsory admission to hospital is commonly known as 'being sectioned'. When you are sectioned three people must agree that this is necessary, including a doctor who knows you.

Community psychiatric nurse
The community psychiatric nurse usually visits people in their own homes. They may support people through difficult times and assist with medication.

Social services
Social sservices can provide services such as home helps, day care services and meals on wheels.

Occupational therapists
These will help people adapt to their environment and everyday life. They may use different types of therapy such as art therapy or music therapy. They may also help to rehabilitate people who have been in hospital.

Counsellors
These will help people identify the problems a person is facing and help discover ways of dealing with them.

Psychiatrists
Will allocate referrals to other members of the team, will have responsibility for a designated number of patients on a hospital ward. Is able to recommend the involuntary detention of a patient in hospital.

Appendix 6
Directory of national mental health services

Name	What is offered	Contact numbers	Website
AnxietyUK (Formerly National Phobics Society)	Help and support if you have an anxiety condition, information and service to professional health care workers. Members' services including: therapy services at reduced rates, members' helpline, bulletin boards & chatrooms	Tel: 08444 775 774 Fax: 0161 226 7727	www.anxietyuk.org.uk Email: info@anxietyuk.org.uk
Depression Alliance	Publications, national network of local self-help groups. Aims to educate public and raise awareness of depression	Tel: 020 7633 0557 Fax: 020 7633 0559	www.depressionalliance.org Email: information@depression alliance.org
Manic Depression Fellowship	Self-help groups, information service. Self-management training courses, employment advice, legal advice line, travel insurance scheme	Tel: 020 7793 2600 Fax: 020 7793 2639	www.mdf.org.uk Email: mdf@mdf.org.uk
Mental Health Foundation	Treatments and strategies, how to get help, news events	Tel: 020 7802 0300 Fax: 020 7802 0301	www.mentalhealth.org.uk Email: mhf@mhf.org.uk
MIND (National Association for Mental Health)	Information, advice and support, local MIND network offering supported housing, crisis helplines, drop-in centres, counselling, befriending, advocacy, employment and training schemes	Tel: 020 8519 2122 Fax: 0208 522 1725 Crisis line: 0845 766 0613 (Mon-Fri 9.15am–5.15pm)	www.mind.org.uk Email: contact@mind.co.uk
Samaritans	Confidential telephone listening service for lonely people with emotional problems who are despairing and suicidal. Some centres have drop-in facilities. Publications, training courses, teaching resources	Tel: 08457 90 90 90 Fax: 020 7375 2162 Crisis line: 0845 790 9090 (24 hour)	www.samaritans.org Email: jo@samaritans.org
Saneline	Out of hours telephone helpline, support during times of crisis, information service, advice on legal rights	Tel: 020 7375 1002 SANEline: 0845 767 8000 Fax: 020 7375 2162	www.sane.org.uk Email: sanemail@sane.org.uk
United Kingdom Council for Psychotherapy	Publications, information, list of local psychotherapists	Tel: 020 7014 9955 Fax: 020 7014 9977	www.psychotherapy.org.uk Email: info@psychotherapy.org.uk

© 2014, *Supporting the Well Being of Girls*, Tina Rae and Elizabeth Piggott, Routledge

References

American Psychological Association (APA) (2007) *Report of the APA Task Force on the Sexualisation of Girls*. New York: APA.

Archer, L., Hutchings, M., Ross, A., Leatherwood, C. & Gilchrist, R. (2003) *Higher Education and Social Class: Issues of Exclusion and Inclusion*, London: Routledge Falmer.

Bartlett, D. (1998) *Stress Perspectives and Processes*. Buckingham and Philadelphia, PA: Open University Press.

BBC News (2012) Many pupils with cancer bullied, charity says. *BBC News*. http://www.bbc.co.uk/news/health-20582967 (accessed 24 February 2014).

Braun, V. & Clark, V. (2006) Using thematic analysis in psychology. *Qualitative Research in Psychology*, 3, 77–101.

British Association for Counselling & Psychotherapy (BACP) (2005) *Counselling and Psychotherapy Resources Directory*. Rugby: British Association for Counselling and Psychotherapy.

Brown, L.M. & Gilligan, C. (1992) *Meeting at the Crossroads: Women's Psychology and Girls' Development*. Cambridge, MA: Harvard University Press.

Cardwell, M. (1996) *Dictionary of Psychology*. Chicago, IL: Fitzroy Dearborn.

Deeley, L. (2008) I'm single, I'm sexy and I'm only 13. *The Times*, July 28.

Department of Health (2011a) *No Health without Mental Health: A Cross-Government Mental Health Outcomes Strategy for People of all Ages*. London: Department of Health.

Department of Health (2011b) *Talking Therapies: A Four-Year Plan of Action*. London: Department of Health.

DfES (Department for Education and Skills) (2001) *Promoting Children's Mental Health within Early Years and School Settings*. London: Department for Education and Employment.

DfES (Department for Education and Skills) (2003) *Every Child Matters: Change for Children in Schools*. London: DfES.

Dunsmuir, S. & Iyadurai, S. (2006) Cognitive behaviour therapy: Effectiveness, expertise and ethics? *DECP Debate*, 122, 15–20.

Eder, D. (1995) *School Talk: Gender and Adolescent Culture*. New Brunswick, NJ: Rutgers University Press.

Fredrickson, B.L. & Roberts, T.A. (1997) Objectification theory: toward understanding women's lived experience and mental health risks. *Psychology of Women Quarterly*, 21, 173–206.

Gow, J. (1996) Reconsidering gender roles on MTV: depictions in the most popular music videos of the early 1990s. *Communication Reports*, 9, 151–161.

Greig, A. (2007) A framework for the delivery of cognitive behaviour therapy in the educational psychology context. *Educational & Child Psychology*, 24(1), 19–44.

Gregory, J., Lowe, S., Bates, C.J., Prentice, A., Jackson, L.V., Smithers, G., Wenlock, R. & Farron, M. (2000) *National Diet and Nutrition Survey: Young People Aged 4 to 18 Years. Volume I: Report of the Diet and Nutrition Survey*. London: The Stationery Office.

Gruerholz, E. & King, A. (1997) Primetime sexual harassment. *Violence Against Women*, 3, 129–148.

Health Professions Council (HPC) (2008) *Standards of Conduct, Performance and Ethics*. London: HPC.

Holmes, J. (2002) All you need is cognitive behaviour therapy? *British Medical Journal*, 324, 288–294.

Kalof, L. (1999) The effects of gender and music video imagery on sexual attitudes. *The Journal of Social Psychology*, 139, 362–378.

Katz, D. & Braly, K. (1933) Racial stereotypes of one hundred college students. *Journal of Abnormal and Social Psychology*, 28, 280–290.

Kilbourne, J. & Lazarus, M. (1987) *Still Killing Us Softly: Advertising's Image of Women*. Mahwah, NJ: Media Education Foundation.

Krassas, N., Blauwkamp, J.M. & Wesselink, P. (2001) Boxing Helena and Corseting Eunice: Sexual rhetoric in Cosmopolitan and Playboy magazines. *Sex Roles*, 44, 751–771.

Krueger, R.A. (1994) *Focus Groups: A Practical Guide for Applied Research*. London: Sage.

Lanis, K. & Covell, K. (1995) Images of women in advertisements: effects on attitudes related to sexual aggression. *Sex Roles*, 32, 639–649.

Layard, R. & Dunn, J. (2009) *A Good Childhood: Searching for Values in a Competitive Age*. London: Penguin Books

Lin, C. (1997) Beefcake versus cheesecake in the 1990s: Sexist portrayals of both genders in television commercials. *Howard Journal of Communications*, 8, 237–249.

Long, R. (2009) *Intervention Toolbox: For Social, Emotional and Behavioural Difficulties*. London: Sage Publications.

MacKay, T. (2002) Discussion paper – the future of educational psychology. *Educational Psychology in Practice*, 18(2), 245–253.

MacKay, T. & Grieg, A. (2007) Editorial. *Educational and Child Psychology*, 24(1), 4–6.

Malamuth, N., Addison, T., & Koss, M. (2000) Pornography and sexual aggression: are there reliable effects and can we understand them? *Annual Review of Sex Research*, 11, 26–91.

Martin, K.A. (1998) Becoming a gendered body: practices in pre-schools. *American Sociological Review*, 63, 494–511.

McKinley, N.M. & Hyde, J.S. (1996) The objectified body consciousness scale. *Psychology of Women Quarterly*, 20, 181–215.

Millward, L. (1995) Focus groups. In Breakwell, G., Hammond, S. & Fife Schaw, C. (eds) *Research Methods in Psychology*, pp. 38–44. London: Sage Publications.

Morgan, D.L. (1998) *The Focus Group Guidebook*. London: Sage Publications.

Nichter, M. (2000) *Fat Talk: What Girls and Their Parents Say about Dieting*, Cambridge, MA: Harvard University Press.

O'Donohue, W., Gold, S.R. & McKay, J.S. (1997) Children as sexual objects: historical and gender trends in magazines. *Sexual Abuse: Journal of Research and Treatment*, 9, 291–301.

Office for National Statistics (2000) *Mental Health in Children and Young People in Great Britain*. London: The Stationery Office.

Office for National Statistics (2013) *Coronary Heart Disease Statistics update – Annual Update November 2013*. https://isdscotland.scot.nhs.uk/Health-Topics/Heart-Disease/Publications/2014-01-28/2014-01-28-Heart-Disease-Summary.pdf?21337527037 (accessed 24 February 2014).

Olweus, D. (1991) Bully/victim problems among schoolchildren: Basic facts and effects of a school based intervention program. In Pepler, D.J. & Rubin, K.H. (eds) *The Development and Treatment of Childhood Aggression*. Hillsdale, NJ: Erlbaum.

Pepler, D.J. & Craig, W.M. (2000) *LaMarsh Research Report # 60*. York University, Toronto: Making a Difference in Bullying.

Plous, S. & Neptune, D. (1997) Racial and gender biases in magazine advertising: historical and gender trends in magazines. *Sexual Abuse: Journal of Research and Treatment*, 9, 291–301.

Pendleton, V. with McRae, D. (2012) *Between the Lines: My Autobiography*. London: HarperSport.

Prever, M. (2006) *Mental Health in Schools*. London: Paul Chapman.

Roberts, R. (1992) *Self-Esteem and Early Learning: Key People from Birth to School*. London: Sage Publications.

Rolon-Dow, R. (2004) Seduced by images: Identity and schooling in the lives of Puerto Rican girls. *Anthropology and Education Quarterly*, 35, 8–29.

Stewart, D. & Shamdasani, P. (1998) Focus group research: exploration and discovery. In Brockman, L. & Rog, D. (eds) *Handbook of Applied Social Research Methods*, pp. 505–527. Newbury Park, CA: Sage.

The Guardian (2008) Call for happiness lessons as teenage depression increases. *The Guardian*, September 10. http://www.theguardian.com/society/2008/sep/10/mental health.happiness (accessed 24 February 2014).

The Guardian (2009) It seems that we can only be interesting if we are smoking, snorting or stabbing. *The Guardian*, 15 April. http://www.theguardian.com/society/2009/apr/15/stereotypes-young-people (accessed 24 February 2014).

The Independent (2012) Get new fathers to stay at home with the baby and we all gain. *The Independent*, 14 May. http://www.independent.co.uk/voices/commentators/mary-ann-sieghart/mary-ann-sieghart-get-new-fathers-to-stay-at-home-with-the-baby-and-we-all-gain-7743402.html (accessed 24 February 2014).

University of East Anglia and National Children's Bureau (2005) *National Evaluation of Children's Trusts: Realising Children's Trust Arrangements, Phase 1 Report*. Cambridge: Institute of Technology.

Vincent, R.C. (1989) Clio's consciousness raised? Portrayal of women in rock videos, re-examined. *Journalism Quarterly*, 66, 155–160.

Ward, L.M. (1995) Talking about sex: Common themes about sexuality in prime-time television programs children and adolescents view most. *Journal of Youth and Adolescence*, 24, 595–615.

Willig, S. & Stainton-Rogers, W. (2003) *The Sage Handbook of Qualitative Research in Psychology*. London: Sage Publications.

Woods, K.A. & Farrell, P.T. (2006) Approaches to psychological assessment by educational psychologists in England and Wales. *School Psychology International* 27(4): 387–404.

World Health Organization (1948) *Constitution of the World Health Organization*. Geneva: World Health Organization.

WriteWork (2008) The effects of bullying. *WriteWork*, 1 February. http://www.writework.com/essay/effects-bullying (accessed 20 February 2014).

Young Hearts & Minds. (2001) *Young Hearts & Minds: Making a Commitment to Children's Mental Health* (Report #161, October 2001). Sacramento, CA: Little Hoover Commission.

Zuckerman, J. & Abraham, R. (2008) *Teenagers and Cosmetic Surgery: Focus on Breast Augmentation and Liposuction*. Washington, DC: National Research Centre for Women and Families.

Index